MARATHON TRAINING
for
Walkers
& Beginners

Fi Hanafiah

D1572663

Published by Revolution Project 2015
Melbourne, Australia

First printing: 2015
ISBN 978-0-9941957-0-8

Book's website: www.marathonwalker.org. To order copies of this
book, please use the contact form at www.marathonwalker.org.

National Library of Australia Cataloguing-in-Publication entry
Creator: Hanafiah, Fi, author.
Title: Marathon Training For Walkers and Beginners / Fi
Hanafiah.
ISBN: 9780994195708 (paperback)
Subjects: Marathon running—Training, Walking (Sports), Health,
Well-being.
Dewey Number: 796.4252

Disclaimer: Please note that the author and the publisher of this
book do not accept any responsibility whatsoever for any error or
omission, nor any loss, injury, damage, adverse outcome or
liability suffered as a result of the information contained in this
book, or reliance upon it. Since the marathon and other
running/walking events can be dangerous and could involve
physical activities that are too strenuous for some individuals to
engage in safely, it is essential that a doctor be consulted before
undertaking training.

This book is dedicated to Andria, Sofie and my parents, Zainab and Rashid.

Preface

I've never been a sporty person. As a kid, I avoided outdoor games. I preferred to sit indoors, at my desk, for hours on end playing computer games. And, unfortunately, this sedentary lifestyle continued well into my adult years.

Not surprisingly, I gained weight steadily – and I was unfit. By age 36, I was 10 kg overweight and I was frequently catching colds and feeling generally rundown. I eventually decided to do something about my health, and came up with the idea of completing a full marathon.

I am not sure why I chose to go from doing very little regular physical activity to committing myself to completing a marathon. Maybe the idea came from a book about setting life goals. Perhaps it was my looming 40th birthday. Either way, I figured it was now or never. So without knowing what I was in for, I decided to try to complete a marathon.

I knew I couldn't run the distance. I had never run further than 10 km. So, I decided I would walk my first marathon. After all, the point was to finish it.

I persuaded my girlfriend to join me, and we trained by taking long walks at night after work. After three months, we walked (or maybe I should say we limped) over the finish line of the inaugural Singapore Sundown Marathon.

It took us slightly more than eight hours and, although I was extremely proud of the achievement, I remembered telling myself during the race that I would never do it again. My body was in pain, particularly my feet. I had chafing and blisters. I slept for 12 hours after the marathon and it took five days for all the aches to go away.

Nevertheless, the marathon changed something in me. Once the aches were gone, my body felt fit and strong. Plus, I enjoyed the race atmosphere, the camaraderie amongst marathoners and the disbelief of my family and friends. So I signed up for another marathon as soon as I could.

For my second marathon, I did some research about footwear and decided to use motion-control shoes. I completed the marathon nearly an hour faster than my first attempt.

For my third marathon, I decided to adopt a more formal training program (three times a week instead of once a week). My time improved by a further 15 minutes.

For my fourth marathon, I read about orthotics and consulted a foot specialist. He said that I had the flattest feet he had ever seen (which explained the foot pain and fatigue), and he ordered custom orthotics for me. My time improved by another 15 minutes, and my feet felt so much better afterwards.

For my fifth marathon, I decided to increase my walking speed. I found myself trying to keep pace with joggers and slower runners. This is when I stumbled upon the advantages of developing a strategy to alternate fast walking and slow walking, which has become my signature method (described later in this book). With the new method, my time improved by nearly 20 minutes.

With each marathon, I have tried and honed new techniques and learnt something new. I have made new friends, travelled to new cities, and my health has gradually improved.

At the time of publishing this book, I have completed more than a dozen full marathons and now weigh 10 kg (22 pounds) less than my peak weight.

I plan to continue to do four or five marathons a year, all completed by walking, with no injuries or over-exertion. My long-term goal is to keep healthy by walking marathons and to complete at least 100 marathons in my lifetime.

In conclusion, I decided to write this book because I truly believe that marathons are for everyone, including non-runners. And, while completing a marathon is a great achievement, I believe lifelong training for multiple marathons done at a relaxed pace can greatly enhance your physical, mental and emotional health.

I call this the 'marathon lifestyle' and I hope you will feel inspired to try it out.

I hope to see you at a marathon some day!

Fi Hanafiah

CONTENTS

1. WHY DO A MARATHON?

It's rewarding on so many levels. Improved health and self-satisfaction are just two of the most significant benefits.

WHY DO A MARATHON?

Picture yourself crossing the marathon finish line, with arms raised in victory and joy. Picture your friends' amazement when you tell them you've completed a marathon – it sounds exciting, doesn't it?

Completing a marathon is beneficial on so many levels: physically, mentally and emotionally. Obviously, losing weight and getting fit are two key benefits, and these two benefits are the motivation for many to take up this pursuit, but there are many more, including:

- **Reducing stress:** Having a bad day? Walking or running it off helps relieve and eliminate the stress that comes with living in today's fast-paced world.

- **Challenging yourself / trying something new:** There are times in everyone's life when daily routine can feel like a blur of boredom. Training for a marathon adds a new element to your life and opens the door to change. Adding more structure to my weekly routine through training has helped me achieve other goals in life too.

- **Being disciplined:** Have you ever avoided starting an exercise regime because you thought you may not stick to it? Most people don't start out as the disciplined person they will soon become once they start training. My tips and techniques will ease you into each phase of training gradually; so much so that if you're concentrating on the training, discipline will be a wonderful by-product. It will show up in other parts of your life as well. For example, any unhealthy eating habits will tend to disappear from your life once you start training.

- **Living longer:** According to a 2013 study[1] by Federation University in Australia, long-distance training can slow down the aging process. The research estimated that long-distance training could add up to 16 years to life expectancy.

- **Bragging rights:** Finishing a marathon is a big achievement. Not many people have done it. For example, according to Running USA in 2013, there were only 541,000 marathon finishers in the US, out of a population of 316 million. There's nothing wrong with blowing your own trumpet a little. It may inspire your friends to try it too.

- **Making new friends:** You are going to interact with many new people and, over time, you may see many of the same people again and again at race events. Friends that you can talk 'marathons' are not easy to find. The training groups and post-event parties can be great fun. It's a community of very passionate people.

- **Supporting good causes:** Many marathon events raise money for charities and worthy causes. While you are participating and getting healthier, you can also be donating money and helping to raise awareness as you support causes that matter to you.

---

[1] *'The effect of exercise on molecular machinery'* led by Prof Fadi Charchar

Myths about marathons

There are many myths or misinformation about marathons. It's time to debunk those myths and prove that they aren't much more than excuses to avoid exercise.

- **Marathon participants are always thin.** It's often the opposite: marathon training is a popular way to get in shape.

- **Marathons are not suitable for women.** Rubbish. Did you know 43% of marathon finishers in 2013 are women, according to Running USA? And, the gap is closing steadily every year.

- **Marathons are for young people.** According to Running USA in 2013, more than 47% of marathon finishers are aged 40 and above. Nearly 20% of marathon finishers are aged 55 and above. People are living, playing and staying physically fit much later in life than in the past.

- **You can't walk in a marathon.** Did you know that most runners will walk some part of a marathon? Walking is a valuable tool to drive away fatigue and to prevent injuries. As you read my training methods, you'll see why this myth is particularly inaccurate.

- **It's unhealthy to walk or run 42 km.** Does that sound like an excuse? It is. Medical research has not made any substantial claims about marathons being hazardous to health, provided you are adequately prepared. Follow the tips and training program in this book and you can avoid injuries and add to your overall health.

- **Marathons are for fast runners only.** This, of course, is just another excuse. Thousands of marathoners clock in finishing times that are hours behind others. For example, approximately 44% of participants take more than six hours to complete the Honolulu Marathon, one of the most popular marathons in the world. No one is left behind. Walkers just need to choose events that allow for the course to remain open long enough to accommodate their personal finishing times, and there are many that do.

DID YOU KNOW?

- Typically, **3-6% of marathon participants walk** instead of run.
- In 2014, the largest marathons were in **New York City (50,403 participants)**, Chicago (40,801 participants) and Paris (39,116 participants).
- Worldwide, there were **4305 marathons in 2014**, with approximately 1.8 million participants.
- The **New York marathon continues to have the highest number of finishers**: 2014: 50,403; 2013: 50,062; 2011: 46,759, 2010: 44,785, 2009: 43,250.
- In 2013, in the US, **females comprised 43% of marathon participants**, compared to 10% in 1980.
- In the US, the **median ages for marathoners are 40 years for males and 36 years for females**.

Walking is a natural place to start

Just like a baby that must crawl before it can walk, I strongly recommend that marathon training starts with walking. Nearly everyone can walk for hours without training, because our bodies are built that way. Those who are already running, but have not yet entered a marathon, may want to take a step back and think about how walking breaks can improve your performance.

Benefits of walking

One of the most important benefits of walking is that there is almost zero chance of injury. I've walked more than a dozen marathons with no injuries whatsoever. This is not surprising, because walking generates far less stress on your body.

Anyone who has suffered multiple injuries from running may also want to consider walking. Who wants to exacerbate an already-worn kneecap or soon-to-be-torn ACL (anterior cruciate ligament) or any number of other injuries begging to happen? Walking allows all of the body parts to get on-board and be in-sync with one another.

Other benefits of walking include:

- **Flexibility**: You can walk near your workplace, your home, even when you're on holiday. And, it doesn't have to be a long walk. Even a five minute walk is beneficial for health.

- **Low-cost**: All you need to buy is a good-fitting pair of shoes and socks. Everything else is optional.

- **Pleasurably healthy**: Walking is one of those rare activities that feels good not only during but *after* the activity is over. As Hippocrates said thousands of years ago: "Walking is man's best medicine".

DID YOU KNOW?
The world's longest running marathons

No.	Marathon name	Location
117	**Boston**	Boston, USA
89	**Yonkers**	Yonkers, USA
89	**Kosice**	Kosice, Slovakia
82	**Polytechnic***	Windsor, UK
69	**Biwa-ko Mainichi**	Otsu, Japan
69	**Belfast**	Belfast, Northern Ireland
68	**Durban Athletic Club***	Durban, South Africa
68	**Kochi**	Kochi, Japan
68	**Jackie Gibson**	Johannesburg, South Africa
68	**Fukuoka**	Fukuoka, Japan

Source: Association of Road Racing Statisticians (as at Dec 2014)
* indicates marathon is no longer held

Before you start

It can be tempting to start training for your marathon straightaway. But doing a marathon properly requires several months of preparation and training, and we will go into that in the next chapter.

2. PREPARATION

Once the prep starts, it gets exciting! You're getting ready for training and that's when you start to realise you can do it.

PREPARATION

See your doctor

Before you start, you need to see your doctor, particularly if:
- You have led a sedentary lifestyle for a long time
- You are overweight
- You have high blood pressure
- You have high cholesterol
- You are a smoker (or recently quit smoking)
- You have a family history of heart problems

Share your proposed marathon training plan with your doctor too (see Chapter 6 for training plans). After your doctor gives his/her ok, get ready to develop your 'physical base'.

Build your 'physical base'

The first question is, can you walk for 60 minutes without stopping? If not, we need to build your physical base (see *Chapter 6: Training plans*). If you aren't there yet, don't stress. Take things one step at a time. If you can walk for 60 minutes at one go, take note of the distance you covered. You can then go ahead with one of the training plans proposed in Chapter 6.

Training Logbook

The whole idea of training is to be able to see an improvement in the distance walked, time taken and your weight. I recommend recording everything in a training diary or logbook. You can also use a smartphone app for logging purposes. See *Chapter 3: Equipment & gear* for suggestions.

Mental preparation

The biggest mental obstacle for beginners is: "Will I be able to finish the marathon?". My advice to you is that a marathon is a journey, not a destination. The benefits of doing a marathon (such as improved fitness and health) come from the training, not by crossing the finish line. If you don't finish the marathon, there is always another marathon to try.

You are a person who has decided to start a new physical activity. Dismiss any concerns about having to be the best. So devote your energy into trying to improve your distance, speed and overall stamina as you move forward. Don't worry about beating others. That may or may not come later.

Emotional preparation

Emotionally, you often need to deal with anxiety and fear. Examples would be fear of injury, fear of not being able to stick to the training plan, fear of letting yourself and your friends down. Not to worry, this book will help you to prepare thoroughly for the marathon and settle those fears.

This may come as a surprise, but participating in marathons has proven to be emotional experiences for some. It's the sheer elation from reaching the finish line that makes grown men and women cry. It is an unforgettable moment and an experience like no other.

Support

Marathon training can be a lonely sport. So, one of the best ways to keep up with this program is to grab a friend or two and make a pact to train together. Training is a great way to stay in touch with friends and share the ups and downs.

As you have heard a thousand times before: practice makes perfect, and perfect can take a while. Having the support from others who are also training will help you over the rough spots as well as provide an additional boost when you're at a high.

Now that you're ready, is everyone else?

You love hanging out with your friends and they enjoy your company too. Your family needs you to help them keep it together every day. Your boss is constantly asking you to come in early or work overtime.

These things will come up, inevitably. It is axiomatic, par for the course and all of those other clichés. So expect it and prepare your strategy in advance so you won't get derailed and frustrated when situations arise. Here are some helpful responses to memorise in order to combat potential social/work distractions that may arise. Being prepared is half the battle, right?

- *"I wish I could, but I have another commitment."*
- *"I'm happy to help. How about if I do it on Tuesday?"*
- *"I'm so grateful for your support. I'll be back later and get right on it."*
- *"You are the best for understanding. This training is so important to me. Let's do brunch after my training on Sunday instead?"*
- *"I can't stay late tonight, but I'm happy to come in early."*
- *"Hey, if you want to hang out, why don't you meet me at the end of my training?"*

Are you ready for your first event?

Once you have built up your stamina and can comfortably walk for 60 minutes continuously, you are ready to find and sign up for a walker-friendly marathon. Finding the right one is very important, particularly if it is your first. Having a great event will reinforce the training program.

Try to find a local marathon, if possible. Go online and conduct a search. Below are some popular websites that list marathon events. Then visit each event's website to compare prices and cut-off times.

RUNNING EVENT CALENDARS

Association of International Marathons and Distance Races (AIMS) calendar (international): **www.aimsworldrunning.com/Calendar.htm**

Runner's World (US): **www.runnersworld.com**

Runner's World (UK): **www.runnersworld.co.uk**

European Calendar: **www.runningcalendar.eu**

Australian Calendar: **www.runningcalendar.com.au**

New Zealand Calendar: **www.runningcalendar.co.nz**

Runner's World (South Africa): **www.runnersworld.co.za**

Run Ireland: **www.runireland.com**

Canadian Running: **runningmagazine.ca**

Here are a few things to consider. First, make sure there is enough time to train for the event. If you are an unfit marathon newbie, don't join a marathon that is less than six months away, unless you love injuries and pain.

Second, you need to check the event's cut-off time. Most marathon events have a cut-off time of six hours, but there will be a few with cut-off times of 6.5 to 8 hours. If you are a marathon newbie and intend to walk at normal pace all the way, try to choose marathons that have a cut-off time that is seven hours or more. The table below shows what pace you should maintain in order to beat the cut-off time.

If the marathon cut-off time is:	You must maintain a pace of at least:	equivalent pace in miles
8 hours	11:22 minutes per km	18:18 minutes per mile
7 hours	9:57 minutes per km	16:01 minutes per mile
6.5 hours	9:14 minutes per km	14:52 minutes per mile
6 hours	8:31 minutes per km	13:43 minutes per mile
5.5 hours	7:49 minutes per km	12:35 minutes per mile
5 hours	7:06 minutes per km	11:26 minutes per mile

If you find that a marathon's cut-off time is too short for your pace, email the organisers to see if they could allow you to start 15 to 30 minutes earlier. This is often allowed in small-scale marathons.

Third, you need to check whether the event is run mainly on road or trails. Road marathons tend to be flat, while trails usually involve more hills and could get muddy after rain. So I would recommend beginners to choose road marathons for their first marathon. Even for road marathons, take note of the inclines and hills ahead of time, to make sure you are prepared.

Fourth, you need to take into account the expected weather during the event. Marathons that take place in hot and humid climates need more training and preparation, and are not recommended for beginners. Marathons are more comfortable when temperatures are between 15 to 20 degrees Celsius.

Half-way into your marathon training, be ready to attempt a half marathon event, which is 21.1 km or 13.1 miles. Before you attempt a half marathon, make sure you can do a 16-18 km walk continuously during training.

Setting goals

Once you have registered for a marathon, you need to set yourself a marathon goal. For beginners, the goal should be to finish the marathon within the cutoff time, without collapsing!

For those who have done a marathon before, set yourself up for a bit of challenge, but be realistic about your goals. For example, it would be very difficult to improve last year's time by more than 30 minutes. Instead, aim for a 10 to 15-minute improvement.

Remember, while you are building up your strength and duration, be kind to yourself and improve at a gradual pace. Follow my training plans (*Chapter 6*) which are all designed to challenge you gradually.

Now let's look at how proper equipment and gear can enhance the enjoyment and safety of your training.

3. EQUIPMENT & GEAR

These items will help make your training regime and marathon experience hassle-free and fun.

EQUIPMENT & GEAR

The right shoes

Shoes are the most important gear for marathoners, regardless of whether you walk or run. Without the right shoes, injuries can happen and the constant discomfort would be tormenting. Yet the choices can be overwhelming.

First, make sure you get to know your feet before you buy your shoes. Are they wide or narrow? Do you have high arches or flat feet? How does your foot strike the ground? Which parts of your shoe soles wear out first?

If you don't know these details, many shoe stores have machines that detect and determine the best type of shoe or if orthotic inserts are needed. Bring a pair of your old shoes so that the store assistants can examine them.

Remember to go to the shoe shop at the end of the day, when your feet are typically expanded. Also wear your frequently-used sports socks when buying the shoes.

- **Running shoes**: Standard running shoes are engineered for heel-to-toe motion, so they can be used for both running and walking. Within the running shoe category, there are a variety of models and manufacturers. It helps to narrow it down before shopping. Although the salespeople may be fully knowledgeable, you don't want to walk out with the latest and most expensive shoes if you don't need them. So plan ahead and do your research.

- **Cross-trainers**: If you engage in other forms of exercise, such as weight training, dance or aerobics, then cross-trainers will be the best choice as an extra pair of shoes for training. They are heavier and are not designed for marathon running/walking, so I would not recommend purchasing these as your main shoe.

- **Orthotics**: You may want to get custom inserts, if you have flat feet or overpronate. They are designed to stabilise the foot and limit motions that might increase joint pain during and after your event. Although there are a few orthotic brands that can be purchased over the counter, custom orthotics are far better in my experience.

- **Sports socks**: Not all socks are created equal. You'll need socks that will help avoid painful blisters and skin irritation. This usually means getting socks that are made of special fibres that wick away sweat and are 'dual-layered' to reduce chafing. Most sporting goods stores should be able to advise you about this. Choosing the right pair can be the difference between pain and pleasure.

Dressing the part

I don't mean fashion. I am talking about practical, functional clothing that will prepare you for anything and everything. When attending an event in a foreign place, check out the forecast in advance and then plan your clothes for weather that is 5°C (approximately 10°F) warmer and cooler than the forecast.

Marathon dressing tips for everyone

Layer your clothing: so you can peel it off as you get warmer. Many marathons now collect discarded clothing and donate them to charity, so wear top layers that you are happy to donate.

Running shorts: come in many different shapes, lengths and designs. Longer styles are commonly preferred for longer distances. Look for shorts made from material that allows the skin to breathe while it wicks away moisture. If possible, look for shorts that have a small pocket (usually at the back). I use that pocket to keep a small plastic ziplock bag filled with jellybeans, chocolate-coated peanuts and salt tablets. Lastly, please follow the washing instructions on the label of your shorts to avoid damaging the fabric.

Short-sleeved shirt or tank top: Some marathoners prefer long-sleeved shirts that they can remove during the race. I maintain that the short-sleeved tank is better for releasing perspiration out into the air rather than back on your skin and clothing, which can cause hyperthermia, chafing and a number of other unpleasant conditions. Avoid cotton materials as they absorb sweat and can become uncomfortable over time. Lastly, please follow the washing instructions on the label of your shirt to avoid damaging the fabric.

Gloves, headbands and hats: Although it's a personal choice, I have found that having all the extras ahead of time can save time and discomfort later. During hot weather, I replace my hat with a sun visor to keep cooler. Remember to always use sunscreen.

Compression tights: These specially-designed tights give leg muscles support, flexion and circulation. Personally, I don't find that they boost my performance, but many marathon participants claim that compression tights reduce soreness, injuries and stiffness. There are different levels of compression, so consider this when shopping.

Arm warmers: Great for cold weather climates, arm warmers provide extra comfort and are also available in compression material. They are perfect for warming up quickly on a cool day. You can always tuck them in your shorts or throw them to a friend on the side of the route when you no longer need them.

For women, a sports bra is a must. Try a few different brands before purchasing to see which provides the most support. Having excellent support, even while training, will eliminate chafing and reduce aches and pains.

Post-marathon clothing: Although they may be exhausted, marathon participants are often up for a celebration afterwards. Be sure to consider which clothes you will want to wear after you have crossed the finish line. Soft terry cloth, velour and other fabrics will feel the best and allow your skin to breath. You will have successfully finished a marathon, after all. It will be time to reward your tired body by wearing something soft and loose.

Gear

Like any sport, being prepared with the right gear is important. Although you don't need to own everything on the list below at the beginning, I recommend getting the items below as soon as possible. The sport is not meant to overwhelm your hip pocket, but as you can see, these items are intended to provide additional comfort, convenience and safety.

- **Running belt**: This is like a tool belt for walkers and runners. A running belt keeps everything you need within reach. My running belt keeps my keys, some cash, a train fare card, phone, earphones, two band-aids (for blisters) and a small energy bar. Most belts come with water bottles and other useful items that attach to the belt; though I tend to leave behind the water bottles since they add weight. If you don't want to wear a belt, consider an armband or running bag.

- **Running bag or fanny pack**: Running bags are not for everyone. But, some walkers enjoy the benefits of having extra water, electrolytes, snacks and gear within easy access. I used a running bag in my earlier marathons because I didn't want to leave out any gear back then. Now that I'm more experienced, I've switched to a running belt to reduce weight. But, if you find you're more comfortable having everything at your disposal, then do it!

- **Sunglasses**: Sheltering your eyes from the sun and other environmental elements is smart. There are wrap-around models, glasses that strap on and other lightweight options specifically for runners or walkers. I use a wrap-around model, which I find very helpful in keeping rain water out of my eyes.

- **Lubricant**: While you might expect occasional blisters on your feet, you may be surprised to find chafing can occur on the groin, inner thighs, nipples and underarms. Athletes' lubricant can help avoid this. A quick and cheap alternative is to use Vaseline or petroleum jelly. I've used Vaseline many times successfully.

Optional gear

The other items on this list are not necessities, but recommended. Like I said earlier, having everything in advance will keep you on track and comfortable. In the beginning, it can be easy to let little things like the weather stop you from advancing your training – so be prepared.

All of these items can be found online or at your local sporting goods store.

- **Rain poncho**: A simple, disposable rain poncho that can be stored in your running bag is ideal. Try it on ahead of time to make sure it doesn't hinder your stride and it covers the areas that make a difference. I've seen some enterprising people using black garbage bags as ponchos too. They just cut holes for their head and arms. Personally, I don't carry a poncho as I like to walk in the rain.

- **Towel**: Buy a quick-dry towel; one that is small, light and intended to quickly absorb sweat. In my earlier marathons, I carried a towel and then used a head sweatband. These days I just use the back of my hand!

Gadgets (optional)

Every sport has its gadgets; walking is no different. Here's a list of some of the latest technological solutions to keep you motivated and avoid the occasional marathon doldrums.

- **GPS watch:** There are several GPS running watches available (some of the most popular brands are Garmin, Polar, Nike and Motorola). These watches will help you make the most of your training. They will record distance, calories burned, pace, speed, steps and more. Some include heart rate monitoring; others have additional functions, such as social media connections and some terrific downloadable multi-sport function apps that you can use to customise your watch. For marathon walkers, make sure the watch has a minimum battery life of eight hours.

- **Smartphone:** If you don't want to get a GPS watch, your own smartphone can be a very good substitute. Most smartphones now have GPS features and can keep track of your training. You can also use the smartphone to play music to keep you motivated during training.

My main concern about using smartphones is their relatively short battery life. Using the GPS features on these phones can run down the battery quickly and you may end up with a useless brick if you take more than six hours to complete your marathon. So, do test the battery life of your smartphone during your training sessions. I used to carry a small battery charging pack in my earlier marathons, in case my smartphone battery ran out.

- **Smartphone apps**: There are so many great apps around, for both Android and iOS smartphones, and new ones come out every year. These are my current favorites:

  - *Runkeeper*: a full-featured, easy-to-use, free app. You can track all outdoor activities on your phone

  - *Noom Weight Loss Coach*: a free app that adds weight loss and nutrition to the mix and help keep track of new habits you're trying to develop; it also has a companion pedometer app called *Noom Walk Pedometer*

  - *Moves Activity Diary*: a free app that constantly tracks how much you walk, run or cycle throughout the day

  - *Endomondo*: a free app that keeps track of duration, distance and speed as its main features; it also has a few other features, such as socialising your training sessions, sending friends pep talks and even tracking hydration

  - *Nike+ Running*: like Endomondo, this app keeps track of your stats and has sharing options as well; and you can set it so you will hear a crowd cheer or have it play a specific song or whatever inspires you

- *MapMyWalk or MapMyRun*: as the name suggests, these apps track your route plus distance, calories, daily nutrition and more; it goes into nutrition and hydration more than the others

- *Strava Running and Cycling*: a tracking app that lets you compare your personal bests with friends and locals

- *Zombies, Run!*: a paid app that turns training into a game, for those of you who like the playful side of sports; almost like being in a video game, Zombies gets you going.

Some of the apps above, e.g. *Runkeeper* or *Noom Weight Loss Coach*, can also be used as a training logbook.

Music players and earphones (optional)

Listening to music or audio books while walking can power you up and keep you going. However, many marathon events discourage the use of earphones for safety reasons. Some even ban the use, so make sure you read the rules and regulations of each event.

The best music gadgets available are compact, water resistant, durable and have a battery life of at least eight hours. Personally, I prefer to use a smartphone as my music player, to minimise the amount of gear that I carry.

Finding the right earphones is getting harder too, as you'll want to consider the various features before buying. Plus, they can be a more expensive than the music players themselves if you're interested in getting the best sound. Personally, I don't think it's necessary to pay top dollar for earphones. They just have to be reasonably waterproof and can stay firmly in your ears during training.

Heart rate monitor (optional)

These usually come with a GPS watch. They are very useful in making sure that we don't over-exert or under-exert ourselves during our training and races.

Chest strap or wristwatch versions are available. The chest strap model is more widely used. The strap fits snugly around the chest and sends the information to a wristwatch-type receiver. The wristwatch-only version is newer, but at this point in time, may not be as accurate as a chest strap model.

> ➢ *All-in-all, we don't really need much gear to get started. The optional gear and gadgets mentioned are more suited for experienced marathoners.*

4. PROPER WALKING TECHNIQUE

Get your walking technique right. It's the foundation for your health and happiness.

PROPER WALKING TECHNIQUE

➤ *"The best way to lengthen out our days is to walk steadily and with a purpose."* – **Charles Dickens**

Any form of physical exercise and movement is important to overall health, particularly as we age. Staying flexible and keeping the joints and muscles working at peak performance will increase your body's ability to stay young.

You will receive these same benefits from either walking or running:
- improved cardiovascular health
- weight loss
- improved sleep
- mood-elevation
- energy boost
- decreased chances of cancer and heart disease.

Walking and running – the differences

Despite debate about which gait is best for weight loss, from my experience both are equally effective.

The biggest difference between walking and running is that during running, both feet are temporarily off the ground. When walking, there is always one foot on the ground at all times. **This difference alone explains why runners are far more prone to injuries than walkers.**

Slow Walking

Walking is considered to be a great overall exercise, as there are many muscle groups used, including muscles in the quadriceps, buttocks and stomach. Many secondary muscles are also used, such as the stabilising group around the pelvis, spine, front of the calves, and the arm and shoulder muscles.

For the purpose of this book, I will refer to the normal sort of walking that everyone does as 'Slow Walking'. So if you end up staying at the Slow Walking stage, it is still an excellent source of regular exercise. Slow Walking is far better than no exercise at all.

In order to maximise the benefits, simply increase the distance and/or length of time spent walking. Slow Walking relies on the body's fat as fuel, which is excellent for weight loss.

Fast Walking

Now I'm going to define 'Fast Walking'. Fast Walking is walking at more than twice the speed of Slow Walking. Fast Walking has the same benefits and calorie-burn as running, if you're doing it right. In order to Fast Walk, take note of the following.

Feet

Fast Walking requires a specific technique in order to make the most of the training. You will end up using your heel and ankle to roll and push. When the heel hits the ground first, the ankle should stay flexed so the foot can roll through the step. Then you will use your toes to give the pushing power. As the one foot is pushing off, the other foot is landing on its heel.

Doing this incorrectly may cause shin splints, so concentrate on maintaining a flexible ankle. Practice the movement until it becomes natural. You will save yourself potential injuries in the future.

➢ *Remember: heel first, flexed ankle, roll through the step, toes push off while other foot descends into the same motion.*

Take care not to lift your feet too high above the ground, because you are wasting energy if you do so. When landing the feet, try to land gently. If you hear your feet thumping loudly on the ground, you're probably landing too hard.

Arms

Our arms affect our walking speed to a surprising extent. My advice for Fast Walking is to bend the arms 90° at the elbow with fists loosely closed. When swinging forward, don't let your fists go above your shoulders. When swinging backwards, don't let fists go behind your hips. Keep your elbows close to your body when swinging and don't let your fists cross the vertical centre line of your chest.

Head and shoulders

You can get upper body aches if your Fast Walking posture is not in check. The head should be level and eyes forward. Elongate your body into a good posture and keep your eyes looking about six metres (20 feet) in front. If you don't follow these basic techniques, your neck and shoulders could experience unnecessary stress and strain.

Back

Keep the back straight and try not to lean forward. Beware: the wrong technique can exacerbate existing back problems.

Stride

One of my most important tips is: **do not over-stride**. Some walkers over-stride to increase their speed, yet it is not efficient. Take smaller steps but quicken your pace. This might sound counterintuitive, but do try it. You will use less energy and increase efficiency with this method.

Cadence (strides per minute)

Increasing walking cadence comes with practice. To give you something to strive for: Olympic race-walkers are coming in at around 200-240 steps per minute.

When I first started marathons, my walking cadence was approximately 120 steps per minute. Then it gradually increased to 130, then 140, then 150 steps per minute. My current Fast Walking cadence is 170 steps per minute, while my Slow Walking cadence is 120 steps per minute.

Breathing

Correct posture has everything to do with the ease with which you breathe while you walk. A quick check for correct posture is something a yoga friend once told me: keep the sternum up toward the sun. He was right. If you follow that advice, your lungs will expand, your shoulders will automatically position themselves correctly and you will increase your overall oxygen intake.

Some might find it helpful to breathe according to their strides. For example, you could breathe in for three strides and breathe out for the next three strides. Personally, I don't breathe according to a fixed rhythm. And it doesn't really matter whether you breathe through your nose or mouth. Do whatever feels natural to you.

Conserving your energy

Over the years, I discovered that one of the most effective techniques for conserving energy during a full marathon is to alternate Fast Walking and Slow Walking. I've developed this into my signature technique and it is something I highly recommend to beginners.

I will delve a bit more into this technique in the next chapter.

5. THE 30/30 METHOD

This method will help you conserve energy and slowly build up stamina.

THE 30/30 METHOD

One of the biggest dangers for first-time marathoners is thinking you have to sprint through to the end. Unless you have been training for a very long time, I can almost guarantee that you will not finish a marathon if you sprint.

This is one reason that I recommend that marathon beginners start with my 30/30 Method, something I've customised and honed over the years.

It's actually very simple. The 30/30 Method means you alternate between Fast and Slow Walking every 30 seconds. In a way, it is a type of interval training, and the method has the following benefits:
- conserves energy
- reduces the potential for injury
- gives your heart and lungs consistent breaks
- gives your legs and feet consistent breaks
- gives you a strategy to maintain motivation
- helps maintain a high average speed and, surprisingly,
- makes faster times more possible.

The basic idea

As mentioned above, the basic idea is simply to alternate Fast Walking and Slow Walking at 30-second intervals. Since this means we do the Fast Walk for 30 seconds and Slow Walk for 30 seconds, I call this doing the '30/30'.

Occasionally I would recommend doing slightly different ratios to suit the circumstances, so 30/30 could morph into 15/45 (Fast Walk for 15 seconds followed by Slow Walking for 45 seconds) or 60/30 or some similar combination.

What is a Fast Walk?

A Fast Walk is a very brisk power walk where your heart rate is elevated to 80-90% of your maximum heart rate[2]. Your breathing will be very audible during a Fast Walk, but not so heavy that you're huffing and puffing. The typical speed for a Fast Walk is 7 to 12 km per hour.

> ➢ *Olympic race walkers can maintain a Fast Walk speed of 14 kilometres per hour over a 50 kilometre distance!*

What is a Slow Walk?

A Slow Walk is a walk done at a comfortable pace; a pace that you can keep up for hours. It is your usual everyday walking pace. You should not be breathing heavily during a Slow Walk. The typical speed for a Slow Walk is 4.5 to 6 km per hour.

---

[2] What is your maximum heart rate? A simple way to calculate this is to subtract your age from 220. So a 40-year-old person's maximum heart rate is 220 minus 40, which equals 180 beats per minute. A more accurate way is to sprint a distance of about 5 km as fast as you can and measure the heart rate immediately after, but do this under supervised medical conditions.

What if I am a runner, not a walker?

If you are a runner, you can still use the 30/30 Method. Simply substitute 'Fast Walking' with 'running' throughout this book. Aim to run fast enough to reach 80-90% of your maximum heart rate.

How to use my 30/30 Method in a marathon

Let's take a look at how to use the 30/30 Method for marathons. If you can master this technique, it may be the key to your marathon success. Here's how you do it.

First, break down the marathon into bite-size pieces.
Imagine the marathon distance is broken down into two kilometres of warm up, followed by four x 10 km legs (2+10+10+10+10=42 km). This makes it less psychologically challenging. After all, most people have done at least one or two 10 km distances before. In addition, each 10 km leg can be treated differently and have different strategies applied to it.

➢ *I call this the '4 x 10 Breakdown'.*

Here's how you use it and the 30/30 Method together.

For less experienced marathoners

- **First 2 km**: Don't sprint out of the gate. Use this as a warm-up. Instead of 30/30, use a 15/45 ratio, i.e. Fast Walk for 15 seconds then Slow Walk for 45 seconds and repeat.

- **Next 10 km**: Continue with 15/45. As a beginner, it is important to resist the urge to speed up at this stage.
- **Next 10 km**: You can start to speed up, i.e. start doing 30/30 in earnest.
- **Next 10 km**: You've finished more than half the marathon. Continue with 30/30 for as long as you can.
- **Last 10 km**: If you're feeling tired, drop to a 15/45 ratio. Otherwise, continue with 30/30. Don't forget to sprint the last 500 metres if you can!

For more experienced marathoners

- **First 2 km**: Don't sprint out of the gate. Use this as a warm-up. Start with 30/30 straightaway.
- **Next 10 km**: Continue using 30/30. Control your desire to speed up too much.
- **Next 10 km**: You can speed up from here. Use a 60/30 ratio, i.e. Fast Walk for 60 seconds then Slow Walk for 30 seconds and repeat.
- **Next 10 km**: You've finished more than half the marathon. Try to achieve a 60/30 ratio for as long as you can.
- **Last 10 km**: If you're feeling tired, do 30/30 again. If you're feeling strong, do as much Fast Walking as you can endure, and do the occasional 30-second Slow Walk to catch your breath. Don't forget to sprint the last 500 metres if you can!

What's my overall speed using the 30/30 Method?

It depends on your Fast Walk speed, your Slow Walk speed and the ratio that you choose. See tables below for examples.

Beginner Walker Fast Walk speed is 7 km/h; Slow Walk speed is 5 km/h		
Fast Walk - Slow Walk ratio	Average speed	Time to finish a marathon at the average speed
15/45 (Fast Walk [FW] 15 secs; Slow Walk [SW] 45 secs)	5.50 km/h	7 hours 40 mins
20/40 (FW 20 secs; SW 40 secs)	5.67 km/h	7 hours 27 mins
30/30 (FW 30 secs; SW 30 secs)	6.00 km/h	7 hours 02 mins
60/30 (FW 60 secs; SW 30 secs)	6.33 km/h	6 hours 40 mins
120/30 (FW 120 secs; SW 30 secs)	6.60 km/h	6 hours 24 mins

Now let's suppose you are a fitter walker and your Fast Walk speed is 9 km/h and your Slow Walk speed is 6 km/h. Then your average speed will be as follows.

Fitter walker Fast Walk speed is 9 km/h; Slow Walk speed is 6 km/h		
Fast Walk - Slow Walk ratio	Average speed	Time to finish a marathon at the average speed
15/45 (Fast Walk [FW] 15 secs; Slow Walk [SW] 45 secs)	6.75 km/h	6 hours 15 mins
20/40 (FW 20 secs; SW 40 secs)	7.00 km/h	6 hours 02 mins
30/30 (FW 30 secs; SW 30 secs)	7.50 km/h	5 hours 38 mins
60/30 (FW 60 secs; SW 30 secs)	8.00 km/h	5 hours 16 mins
120/30 (FW 120 secs; SW 30 secs)	8.40 km/h	5 hours 01 mins

How do you know when to Fast Walk and when to Slow Walk?

The easiest way is to use smartphone apps. These apps will vibrate or make sounds at the appropriate time to tell you when to Fast Walk and when to Slow Walk. Do a search for 'interval timer' on the Android or Apple app stores. For Android phones, there are free apps, such as *HIIT Interval Training Timer* or *Run Walk Intervals*. For Apple iOS phones, there is a free app called *Interval Timer*.

How do I ensure my walk speeds are consistent?

Generally, you can do this by monitoring how heavy you are breathing. Your Slow Walks should be feel relaxed, while your Fast Walks should involve fast, audible breathing. Do note that if you're huffing and puffing during a Fast Walk, it means you're going too fast. Slow down a notch.

For the technologically inclined, you can use smartphone apps that function as a metronome to maintain a specific cadence or strides per minute. For example, you can set the metronome app to 150-180 beats per minute, and match your strides or cadence to it during Fast Walks. During the Slow Walk part, simply ignore the metronome and walk at a relaxed pace. To find these metronome apps, do a search for *'Mobile Metronome'* or simply *'metronome'* on the Android or Apple app stores. There are plenty of free metronome apps available.

Alternatively you could choose fast songs or speed up your favourite songs so that they have the desired tempo. I use an open source software called 'Audacity' (available on Windows, Mac and Linux) to speed up my songs to the correct tempo.

How do I decide which ratio to choose, and which pace to walk?

It depends on your level of fitness and experience. If you have never done a marathon before and you're not sure you can even finish, use a 15/45 Fast Walk - Slow Walk ratio and stick to that as far as you can. When you finally run out of energy, walk to the finish in the final few kilometres. If you are very experienced, use a 120/30 Fast Walk - Slow Walk ratio to set your marathon pace and adjust accordingly during the race.

What if I start feeling tired?

Do more frequent and longer Slow Walks. Decrease your ratio to a 15/45 Fast Walk – Slow Walk or even 10/50 if necessary. Then slowly increase the duration of Fast Walks when your fatigue goes away.

Can I shorten my Slow Walk time to less than 15 seconds to get a faster overall speed?

Generally, the Slow Walk time should be at least 30 seconds. If it is shorter than 30 seconds you may not have enough time to get your breath back, and this quickly becomes a vicious cycle. To go faster, lengthen the Fast Walking time while keeping the Slow Walking time to at least 30 seconds.

What tips do you have for doing the Fast Walk?

First, use short strides and a fast cadence for the Fast Walk (see if you can do 150-180 strides per minute). Don't lengthen your stride to go faster, you could get injured.

Second, don't lift your feet too high above the ground and try to land gently on the ground. Imagine you are walking barefoot on very hot sand and are trying to get away quickly without touching the sand too much!

> ➤ *There have been many times when fatigue or blisters have made me doubt whether I could complete a marathon race. But, applying my 30/30 Method has worked for me every single time. That's why I'm sharing it with you.*

6. TRAINING PLANS

There's more than one way to train—check out the concepts and options to work what's best for you.

TRAINING PLANS

Start by determining your goals

Not every marathon participant enters a race to win. In fact, those who run competitively comprise a very small percentage of participants.

There are many reasons why people take up walking or running, so never feel that your goals have to match another's or that this must be competitive.

- **Finishing**: Anyone who has already finished a marathon can tell you that it is life-changing. If it is your first marathon, then I recommend that you concentrate on making it across the finish line as your primary goal. Don't worry too much about how long it takes. You will still be able to say you have completed a marathon! Making it across without injuries or drama is an enhanced version of the same goal.

- **Realistic time goals**: If you are embarking on your first marathon, don't worry about setting a time goal. If you insist, then make sure the goal you set is realistic. First time marathoners might expect a time of anywhere from four to six hours for runners and six to eight hours for walkers. One rule of thumb is to multiply your 10 km time by 5 to get a reasonable time goal for beginners. If you are an experienced walker or runner, multiply your 10 km time by 4.5.

- **Pace goals**: You can also set a goal to walk at a specific pace. Setting a pace goal is more about how fast you are finishing each km/mile. For example, if you try to go under eight minutes and 30 seconds every kilometre, you would finish the marathon in less than six hours.

- **Qualifying goals**: Some races require meeting a qualifying goal to enter. Generally, that includes races that are intended for the very experienced walker or runner.

Where to train

 The main point I want to make here is that in order to support your new sport and habits, you have to make it something that is easy to do regardless of the circumstances. Consider the following when planning your training.

- **Safety**: Safety is first and foremost. Use your common sense and remember that it is not smart to veer off trails, walk alone in secluded areas or off road where wild animals might be living. Beware of training during times of low visibility too, e.g. at night or in bad weather.

- **Surface**: It is good to train on a variety of surfaces and elevations that will be similar to your marathon route. Start easy and select a smooth, flat course. You'll want to increase your fitness level before going on uneven or off-road terrains. It's important to remember that you will experience different results on various terrains, so don't be hard on yourself. Remember that road or pavement surfaces will tire your legs more quickly, so you will need to build your endurance if your event's route has lots of road running.

- **Convenience**: Your training will be more consistent when the location is convenient. If having to drive to the training destination is going to be a deterrent, then select a location that is within walking distance. Or create a course that starts from the road in front of your house or workplace.

- **Weather**: If you live in an area with more extreme weather conditions, make sure you have some alternatives ready, such as a gym or a treadmill at home. If the weather is somewhat unpredictable, always carry a poncho or extra layers of clothing to be prepared.

When to train

- **Time between workouts**: Recommendations vary, but my rule of thumb is to schedule a 48-hour downtime period between strenuous training. Why? Because that is how long it takes for your muscles to fully recover from such strenuous use, especially if you are older. If you honour your body, it will work for you. In fact, it will excel and provide peak performance levels without injuries if you take care of it all along the way. So plan your training and workouts accordingly.

- **Time of day**: There is a lot of research on the subject of best time of the day for exercise. The reality is that time of day depends on your schedule and whether you're at your best in the morning, afternoon or evening. Most importantly, the main idea is to select the time of day that will allow training consistency. The goal with all of this planning is to avoid what may seem to be valid reasons for opting out. Success depends on planning ahead on all of these details.

- **Use the Weekends**: At first, it may be tempting to rest during the weekend, but you may find that weekends are best for long duration training. More likely, it is when you have the most free time, so you can get serious about your training. I suggest using one weekend day for your long runs.

- **Weather**: The very best weather conditions for marathon training is when the temperature is on the cool side. Ideal weather will depend partially on your fitness level, as the leaner and less fat content of your body, the longer it will take to warm up. Starting out cool with a little humidity is the most perfect for breathing and overall comfort. Personally, I like temperatures around 17°C (63°F) with relative humidity around 60%. As always, have an alternative plan in case the weather is not agreeable.

Warming up and stretching

There are many schools of thought on warming up and stretching, before or after training. For me, a minimal amount of light stretching before training is usually enough. Then for a warm up, I simply start walking at a slow pace that gradually gets faster. The important thing to know is that every individual's body has different warm up and stretching needs, and you need to find a routine that works for you.

Example warm ups and stretches

- **Walk around lunge-style**: Make sure your thighs and knees are perpendicular with your calves. Knees should never be ahead of the foot. Shake out legs afterwards. Proper form is important.
- **Isometric stretches for each muscle group**: Hold for 30-60 seconds. Repeat a few times per muscle group. Don't lock up your knees.
- **Butt kicks**: Stand tall and alternate back kicks that reach your glutes. Stretches the quads and the glutes.

- **Toy soldier**: Keep arms and legs straight. Flex toes and kick legs out in front, one at a time. Alternate arms.
- **Walk slowly for 5 minutes (my preferred method)**: Give every part of your body a chance to loosen up and bring up your heart rate slowly.
- **Skipping for 1-3 minutes**: A childlike pleasure, skipping is good for the heart and warms up the whole body.
- **Backward jogging**: Great for conditioning different parts of the legs. Start with 40-50 metre distances.
- **Shuffle sidestep**: Step to the right and then to the left, then back to the right. You can do this walking or jogging and build up the intensity while moving quickly. It's almost a dance.

Cross-training

Doing your best marathon requires some cross-training. One of the most enjoyable parts of incorporating other sporting activities into your training regime is that it will be a nice respite from walking or running. Additionally, cross-training can enhance your marathon training by strengthening weak areas, such as the back, ankles and knees.

Consequently, it will help you avoid injuries from over-use. It will also stabilise your muscle groups by strengthening those that are not as engaged when walking or running. Overall, it will increase your endurance and performance.

Schedule your cross-training at least 48-hours before or after your longest training session in the week.

Cross-training suggestions

You will have your own favorites, but here are a few activities to consider including in your marathon training:

- Climbing
- Cycling
- Swimming
- Rowing
- Martial arts
- Elliptical trainer
- Yoga

Weight or strength-training

Another good type of cross-training is weight-training. Weight-training strengthens both muscles and bones, which makes it critical for marathon training. Imagine how long it would take to strengthen your body with running or walking alone.

I recommend weight-training once per fortnight. By doing these ancillary workouts your ability to finish a marathon without injuries will be at an all time high.

The goals are the same for all cross-training. You are strengthening muscles, bones and stabilising the entire body. Believe it or not, all of these extra workouts will help increase your speed.

Speed training or tempo runs

Speed training entails going faster than your target marathon pace by 15-30 seconds faster per km. You should try to keep up this pace for 30 minutes.

This type of training improves your body's ability to process oxygen, basically improving your 'gas mileage'. Remember that as you go faster, try not to over-stride. Instead, quicken your cadence (strides per minute).

Hill training

Training on hills strengthens your leg muscles and improves your cardiovascular system. Remember to take shorter strides as you go up and down, and don't lean forward or back, but keep the posture upright.

You must be especially careful when going downhill because the probability of getting an injury or severe muscle soreness is high (I have personal experience of this). Do not sprint, instead shorten your strides. Step lightly and listen out to make sure your feet don't hit the ground hard with a 'slapping' sound.

You should do hill training every two weeks or so. Don't do more than one hill training per week.

Treadmill training

As a rule, I don't usually recommend using a treadmill for marathon training; mostly because it does not provide the proper terrain and does not provide scenery to stimulate and motivate the mind.

However, for my second marathon I did most of my training indoors on a treadmill as I was living in Singapore and found outdoor exercise very uncomfortable in the high humidity. At other times I have been working long hours, travelling a lot for work, and found training at home or in hotel gyms was the only way to maintain a regular training routine. You do the best you can with what you've got.

I have included this section as I want to make sure you know how to get the most from treadmill training, should you find yourself in similar situations.

Owning or having access to a treadmill is actually an advantage for a few reasons. First, it allows you to train in bad weather conditions. Second, you can set your training difficulty level easily. Third, a treadmill makes it easy to train at a specific speed.

As you improve, you will want to train on terrain that is close to that which you will find on the upcoming event course.

Tips for treadmill training

- **Don't overdo it**: Train the same as you would if you were outdoors. Gym goers can get competitive while racing on a treadmill. Focus on your training, not your fellow gym goers.

- **Work on your cadence**: Focus on your footwork and timing. See if you can increase the amount of times your feet hit the treadmill in one minute. Can you reach 150-180 steps per minute? Experiment. Work up to 1% incline: Start with zero incline and when you are ready, train at 1% incline. No need to raise the incline further. There's no advantage to getting calf-strain.

Training plans

Alright, here comes the crucial part of your marathon training. You need to pick a training plan that is suitable for you and stick to it as much as you can.

It's okay to miss one or two sessions; you don't have to make up for them. But, try not to miss the long distance sessions each week. If you miss the longest distance session in your training plan (which are 32 km for beginners), I strongly recommend you find time to make up that session within a few days.

How the Training Plans are designed

All Training Plans start with shorter distances to ease you into the program. All Training Plans have one long distance session each week. This long distance is gradually increased approximately 10% every week until it reaches a maximum distance approximately 2-3 weeks before your scheduled marathon event. After this peak, there is a tapering period where you rest and build up your strength.

I have also taken into account that everybody has a busy schedule. Therefore, I have only scheduled three sessions a week. Whereas many other training programs may advocate five or even six training sessions a week, my experience over the years has shown that three sessions are sufficient to build you up for a marathon.

How to read the Training Plans

Each Training Plan is organised by the week. Each week has three training sessions: two short sessions and one long distance session. Most people would do the long distance session during the weekend, where there is more free time. So a typical week could look like this:

- Tuesday: short session (30 minutes)
- Thursday: short session (30 minutes)
- Saturday: long distance session.

You should have a gap of at least 48 hours between the long distance session and the short session following it, to allow your body to recover. It doesn't matter if you do the long distance session in the beginning of the week or in the middle, as long as you do all three training sessions each week.

How fast should I go during the training sessions?

For the short sessions, go at your target marathon pace. Every two weeks or so, do a speed session where you go about 15-30 seconds faster per km than your target marathon pace.

Occasionally, substitute your speed sessions with hill training. This entails finding a gentle slope that is long enough for you to walk up for at least one minute continuously, and then repeatedly going up and down the slope.

For long distance sessions that are 20 km or less, you can go at your target marathon pace as well.

For long distance sessions that are more than 20 km, go at a pace that is 30-60 seconds slower per km than your target marathon pace. So, if you target marathon pace is 8:00 mins/km, then your pace during these extra long distance sessions should be between 8:30 mins/km and 9:00 min/km.

Can I incorporate other activities in my training?

Definitely! You may have already read earlier in this chapter about cross-training. This means doing something other than walking to exercise and strengthen other parts of the body.

➢ *Every two weeks or so, you should replace one of your short sessions with cross-training.*

Do I use the 30/30 Method during training?

Absolutely, training is the time to experiment with different Fast Walk - Slow Walk ratios. I started with a 30/30 ratio, and tried various combinations such as 15/45, 60/30 and so on to suit different paces.

As for runners, I suggest you still try the 30/30 Method, but replace the Fast Walk portions with running instead. You will still benefit in terms of conservation of energy and injury prevention.

What if I don't have time to do two short sessions every week?

I strongly recommend that you use your day-to-day activities as opportunities to walk, e.g. walk to the grocery store and back. A brisk 15-minute walk to the store and a brisk 15- minute walk back are as good as 30 minutes in the gym.

Shouldn't long distance sessions continuously increase in distance?

The changing distances over time (long, then shorter, then longer again) provide a mini recovery stage between peak distances. This will help to reduce injuries.

Select your training plan

Select the Training Plan (TP) that suits you

- TP1 (Beginner 1):   "I can't walk very far at all'"

- TP2 (Beginner 2):   "I can walk at least 5 km, but I'm not in shape."

- TP3 (Beginner 3):   "I'm fit, but I've never done a marathon."

- TP4 (Intermediate):   "I've done one or two marathons and I want to improve my time."

- TP5 (Advanced):   "I've done many marathons."

- TP6 (Advanced+):   "I want to embrace the marathon lifestyle."

TP1: Beginner 1

"I can't walk very far at all."

If you don't do much walking at all, check to see if you can complete the activities in the preparation plan below.

If you can't walk continuously for 60 minutes by Week 8, don't worry. Take a few more weeks to reach that goal. It doesn't matter if it takes twice as long to be able to walk continuously for 60 minutes, what matters is that you are building a foundation level of fitness for your future walks.

PREPARATION PLAN	8 WEEKS
Week 1	Walk slowly for 10 minutes (twice a week)
Week 2	Walk slowly for 15 minutes (twice a week)
Week 3	Walk slowly for 20 minutes (twice a week)
Week 4	Walk slowly for 25 minutes (twice a week)
Week 5	Walk briskly for 30 minutes (twice a week)
Week 6	Walk briskly for 40 minutes (twice a week)
Week 7	Walk briskly for 50 minutes (twice a week)
Week 8	Walk briskly for 60 minutes (twice a week)

Note: If you find the above plan easy from the outset, jump to Week 8 and see if you can walk for 60 minutes. If you can do it, continue with TP1 below. If you find the above plan a bit difficult, stretch it out to 16 weeks or more, increasing your walking time only when you are ready to do so.

○ **Cross-training or strength-training**: There's no need for cross-training at this point, but do take the stairs at every opportunity.

Once you have completed the eight-week preparation training, you can embark on the next 26 weeks as follows:

Training Plan 1: BEGINNER 1						26 WEEKS	
Week	Short Session (minutes)		Long Session	Week	Short Session (minutes)		Long Session
	1	2	km (miles)		1	2	km (miles)
1	30	30	5 km (3.1)	14	30	30	20 km (12.4)
2	30	30	6 km (3.7)	15	30	30	22 km (13.7)
3	30	30	7 km (4.3)	16	30	30	24 km (14.9)
4	30	30	8 km (5.0)	17	30	30	26 km (16.2)
5	30	30	9 km (5.6)	18	30	30	20 km (12.4)
6	30	30	10 km (6.2)	19	30	30	28 km (17.4)
7	30	30	11 km (6.8)	20	30	30	20 km (12.4)
8	30	30	12 km (7.5)	21	30	30	30 km (18.6)
9	30	30	13 km (8.1)	22	30	30	20 km (12.4)
10	30	30	14 km (8.7)	23	30	30	32 km (20.0)
11	30	30	15 km (9.3)	24	30	30	20 km (12.4)
12	30	30	16 km (10.0)	25	30	30	12 km (7.5)
13	30	30	18 km (11.2)	26	30	30	Marathon!

⊙ **Speed sessions or hill training**: Incorporate these into your short sessions every two weeks or so.

⊙ **Practice race**: Register for a half-marathon that takes place during the middle of the training plan (around weeks 14-16).

⊙ **Cross-training or strength-training**: Replace one short session with cross training at least once every two weeks.

TP2: Beginner 2

"I can walk at least 5 km, but I'm not in shape."

Many people can go the distance, but not at a pace that encourages improvement. This plan builds stamina and speed. You'll start getting in shape by following this simple regimen.

Training Plan 2: BEGINNER 2							24 WEEKS
Week	Short Session (minutes)		Long Session	Week	Short Session (minutes)		Long Session
	1	2	km (miles)		1	2	km (miles)
1	30	30	6 km (3.7)	13	30	30	22 km (13.7)
2	30	30	7 km (4.3)	14	30	30	24 km (14.9)
3	30	30	8 km (5.0)	15	30	30	26 km (16.2)
4	30	30	9 km (5.6)	16	30	30	20 km (12.4)
5	30	30	10 km (6.2)	17	30	30	28 km (17.4)
6	30	30	11 km (6.8)	18	30	30	20 km (12.4)
7	30	30	12 km (7.5)	19	30	30	30 km (18.6)
8	30	30	13 km (8.1)	20	30	30	20 km (12.4)
9	30	30	14 km (8.7)	21	30	30	32 km (20.0)
10	30	30	16 km (10.0)	22	30	30	20 km (12.4)
11	30	30	18 km (11.2)	23	30	30	12 km (7.5)
12	30	30	20 km (12.4)	24	30	30	Marathon!

✪ **Speed sessions or hill training**: Incorporate these into your short sessions every two weeks or so.

✪ **Practice race**: Register for a half-marathon race that takes place during the middle of the training plan (Weeks 12-14).

✪ **Cross-training or strength-training**: Replace one short session with cross training at least once every two weeks.

TP3: Beginner 3

"I'm fit, but I have never done a marathon."

This 20-week training plan will ease you into the marathon distance.

Training Plan 3: BEGINNER 3						20 WEEKS	
Week	Short Session (minutes)		Long Session	Week	Short Session (minutes)		Long Session
	1	2	km (miles)		1	2	km (miles)
1	30	30	6 km (3.7)	11	30	30	26 km (16.2)
2	30	30	8 km (5.0)	12	30	30	20 km (12.4)
3	30	30	10 km (6.2)	13	30	30	28 km (17.4)
4	30	30	12 km (7.5)	14	30	30	20 km (12.4)
5	30	30	14 km (8.7)	15	30	30	30 km (18.6)
6	30	30	16 km (10.0)	16	30	30	20 km (12.4)
7	30	30	18 km (11.2)	17	30	30	32 km (20.0)
8	30	30	20 km (12.4)	18	30	30	20 km (12.4)
9	30	30	22 km (13.7)	19	30	30	12 km (7.5)
10	30	30	24 km (14.9)	20	30	30	Marathon!

❂ **Speed sessions or hill training**: Incorporate these into your short sessions every two weeks or so.

❂ **Practice race**: Register for a half-marathon race that takes place during the middle of the training plan (Weeks 9-11).

❂ **Cross-training or strength-training**: Replace one short session with cross training at least once every two weeks.

TP4: Intermediate

"I've done one or two marathons and I want to improve my time."

So you are ready to beat your time. This plan will build on your past experiences and current fitness level.

Training Plan 4: INTERMEDIATE					16 WEEKS		
	Short Session (minutes)		Long Session		Short Session (minutes)		Long Session
Week	1	2	km (miles)	Week	1	2	km (miles)
1	30	30	10 km (6.2)	9	30	30	30 km (18.6)
2	30	30	14 km (8.7)	10	30	30	20 km (12.4)
3	30	30	18 km (11.2)	11	30	30	32 km (20.0)
4	30	30	22 km (13.7)	12	30	30	20 km (12.4)
5	30	30	24 km (14.9)	13	30	30	34 km (21.1)
6	30	30	26 km (16.2)	14	30	30	20 km (12.4)
7	30	30	28 km (17.4)	15	30	30	12 km (7.5)
8	30	30	20 km (12.4)	16	30	30	Marathon!*

The day before the marathon: do a 20-minute session to loosen up

Note: Week 13 has a crucial 34 km session. This will toughen your legs and mentally prepare you for a faster marathon time. Your risk of injury is high during this long session so go 30-60 seconds slower per km than your target pace.

○ **Speed sessions or hill training**: Incorporate these into your short sessions every two weeks or so.

○ **Practice race**: Register for a half-marathon race that takes place during the middle of the training plan (Weeks 5-7).

○ **Cross-training or strength-training**: Replace one short session with cross training at least once every two weeks.

TP5: Advanced

"I've done many marathons."

This 12-week plan is ideal for anyone who has participated in many marathons, but hasn't trained for 3 or 4 months.

Training Plan 5: ADVANCED			12 WEEKS
Week	Short Session 1	Short Session 2	Long Session
1	30 mins	30 mins	14 km (8.7 miles)
2	30 mins	30 mins	18 km (11.2 miles)
3	30 mins	30 mins	22 km (13.7 miles)
4	30 mins	30 mins	26 km (16.2 miles)
5	30 mins	30 mins	30 km (18.6 miles)
6	30 mins	30 mins	20 km (12.4 miles)
7	30 mins	30 mins	32 km (20.0 miles)
8	30 mins	30 mins	20 km (12.4 miles)
9	30 mins	30 mins	34 km (21.1 miles)
10	30 mins	30 mins	20 km (12.4 miles)
11	30 mins	30 mins	12 km (7.5 miles)
12	30 mins	30 mins	Marathon!*

The day before the marathon: do a 20-minute session to loosen up

Note: Week 9 has a crucial 34 km session. This will toughen your legs and mentally prepare you for a faster marathon time. Your risk of injury is high during this long session so go 30-60 seconds slower per km than your target pace.

✪ **Speed sessions or hill training**: Incorporate these into your short sessions every two weeks or so.

✪ **Practice race**: Register for a half-marathon race that takes place during the middle of the training plan (Weeks 3-5).

✪ **Cross-training or strength-training**: Replace one short session with cross training at least once every two weeks.

TP6: Advanced+

"I want to embrace the marathon lifestyle."

The following 'marathon lifestyle' training plans prepare you for multiple marathons all-year long.

If you don't know when you're going to do your next marathon, follow this three-week cycle and repeat. It maintains your fitness and gets you ready to switch to a more specific training plan when you decide on the date of your next marathon.

Training Plan 6: ADVANCED+			3-WEEK CYCLE
Week	Short Session 1	Short Session 2	Long Session
1	30 mins	30 mins	16 km (10.0 miles)
2	30 mins	30 mins	20 km (12.4 miles)
3	30 mins	30 mins	24 km (14.9 miles)

○ **Speed sessions or hill training**: Incorporate these into your short sessions at least once per three-week cycle.

○ **Cross-training or strength-training**: Replace one of your short sessions with cross training at least once per three-week cycle.

"What if I want to do a marathon every eight weeks?"

Let's assume you did a marathon on the weekend. Immediately after that weekend, follow this eight-week training plan.

Training Plan 6: ADVANCED+			8-WEEK CYCLE
Week	Short Session 1	Short Session 2	Long Session
1	30 mins	30 mins	Rest
2	30 mins	30 mins	14 km (8.7 miles)
3	30 mins	30 mins	18 km (11.2 miles)
4	30 mins	30 mins	22 km (13.7 miles)
5	30 mins	30 mins	26 km (16.2 miles)
6	30 mins	30 mins	32 km (20.0 miles)
7	30 mins	30 mins	20 km (12.4 miles)
8	30 mins	30 mins	Marathon!*

* The day before the marathon: do a 20-minute session to loosen up

✪ **Speed sessions or hill training**: Incorporate these into your short sessions every two weeks or so.

✪ **Cross-training or strength-training**: Replace one short session with cross training at least once every two weeks.

"What if I want to do a marathon every month?"

Ironically, doing a marathon every month would not require that much training, as your fitness is maintained at a consistently high level.

Training Plan 6: ADVANCED+			4-WEEK CYCLE
Week	Short Session 1	Short Session 2	Long Session
1	30 mins	30 mins	Rest
2	30 mins	30 mins	14 km (8.7 miles)
3	30 mins	30 mins	22 km (13.7 miles)
4	30 mins	30 mins	Marathon!*

The day before the marathon: you can do a 20 minute session to loosen up

❂ **Speed sessions or hill training**: Incorporate these into your short sessions every two weeks or so.

❂ **Cross-training or strength-training**: Replace one short session with cross training at least once in the four weeks.

Conclusion

In the beginning, there was a plan. But the best laid plan is one that is customised to your lifestyle, body, endurance and goals. So I encourage all new walkers and runners to use the months of training to experiment with every facet of the sport. The earlier you start, the more time you will have to test out what works best for your progress.

> ➤ *Training is the time to experiment with your nutrition, clothing, gear and training locations.*

This is the time to go all out and find out what makes your marathon training tick. Maybe it's the music you listen to or the friend you buddy with, finding the right combination of assets will be the key to your enjoyment and success.

7. TRAINING MOTIVATION

Inspiration, motivation, the right attitude and mindset — all combine to make it work.

TRAINING MOTIVATION

Staying committed to the program

Staying committed to any workout program can be tough; staying on course with a program that continuously challenges you is going to be tougher.

What is your personality type? Are you someone who embarks on a new project by first buying all the equipment, trying it out for a few days and then finds a reason not to go any further? Are you determined to complete what you start?

If you are fortunate to have a burning desire and solid determination, you may not need to read this chapter, but for the rest of us, it pays to have a strategy.

In this chapter, I'm helping you to prepare for how you are going to handle yourself on those days when you just don't feel like it or your body feels a little tired and sore. It happens to the best of us. So we all must have a plan.

> ➢ *Here are some strategies/tactics to help everyone overcome the marathon doldrums. Mix and match or select those you know will work. The goal is to plan ahead, so don't wait!*

Put yourself out there

One way to step on the road of no return is to tell everyone you know about your new sport, intentions and goals. The more people you tell, the better. There are a few reasons for this. First: for support. Imagine having everyone you know asking about your progress and cheering you on.

Second: once you've told everyone and they begin asking about your progress, you will want to make sure there has been progress for fear of looking like a failure. It's not that your friends will shame you if you fail, but you will want to prove that you are not 'all talk'.

While you're at it, hand pick your cheering squad. Observe which members of your close groups are genuinely happy and supportive. Make a mental note of the naysayers and stay away.

- **Cheerleaders**: Now you know who will be and who won't be your natural cheerleading squad. This will come in handy when it's time to walk or run any of your races, especially your first. Having a support group will be a big deal as you progress. On those mornings where you just don't want to get up and go, remind yourself you have cheerleaders who would be happy to intervene and help to get you motivated again.

- **The buddy system**: Having a friend or two along during training is possibly the easiest motivation. Or join a marathon training group, which is just more of the same. Both will provide a sense of belonging and responsibility to keep it up.

The biggest advantage is obvious: you and your mates can help one another to stay motivated. Here are some examples of the benefits of sharing your training journey with others:

- sharing tips on where to get gear
- select destination races and go together
- others can keep an eye on your form
- being with like-minded others is fun
- you will be far less likely to miss a training session if others are involved
- sharing tips on techniques and discoveries.

In fact, athletes often say they improve faster when working out with others.

Training logbook or diary

I mentioned this earlier when discussing gear and preparation. You'll want to keep track of your stats as it is vital to your improvement. It is like a daily weigh-in when on a diet. The numbers don't lie. Without the numbers, it is easy to deceive yourself and measure your performance by your physical condition.

There are several ways to keep a log. We've already gone into using a GPS watch, phone, computer software or a website. Equally effective is a paper notebook that you put in the same place every day so you don't forget to record your stats. It's definitely low-tech and low-cost, but works just as well.

The only thing that counts is that you realise the importance of recording the information on a daily basis.

Blood sugar levels

Did you know your nutrition affects your motivation? Low blood sugar can lead to a lack of energy and motivation. So maintain your blood sugar levels with regular snacks of fruit, muesli, energy bars and the like. Do this before, during and after training.

More motivational tips

Don't panic if you end up missing a training session or two. I can pretty much guarantee that there hasn't been an athlete who has not missed some training sessions along the road. Don't beat yourself up.

The important thing is making sure you get 'back on the horse'. You're already well on your way to having your training become a habit, so don't let these little hiccups get you down.

In general, I think there is no need to make up for missed training. Just move on to the next training session on your training plan.

The only exception, and I've mentioned this before in *Chapter 6*, is the long slow distance that is scheduled once a week in all the training plans. Please, please, try not to miss the long slow distances, particularly the longest one in your training plan.

For marathon beginners, the long slow distances (particularly the 32 km session) are vital in strengthening your legs and boosting your confidence. If you miss a long slow distance session on the weekend, try to make up for it within the next three days.

- **Self-talk/mantras**: Mind training is just as important as training the body. For example, most brains are trained to see the positive sides of things and people, some see the negative. Most people flow in and out of both, depending on everything else that is happening in their lives.

  A huge benefit of marathon training is that you will be less susceptible to other's moods and negativity because as you become stronger, your resolve and upbeat attitude will increase. But still, we have to prepare ourselves for those few down times, that will be far and few between (we hope).

- **Pep talks**: On many occasions, I have had to give myself pep talks and pick-me-ups. My pep talks are the ones where I tell myself how great I'm going to feel after accomplishing this and what incredible training this is for all parts of myself: body, mind, spirit. I think confident thoughts and become my own cheerleader.

- **Pick-me-ups**: These are what I use when my body feels achy and tired and I'm worried that I might not be able to go on. I give myself refreshers, like water, a snack or change the music. I save special water with electrolytes, favorite snacks and music that makes me forget about any aches and pains.

- **Mantras**: A mantra is a word or phrase, that when used over and over puts your mind into a meditative state. The purpose of the meditative state is that it shuts off the babble that runs through your brain causing us to think about anything and everything. Using a mantra will help ensure you won't be thinking about the twitch on your left foot or the sweat that is chafing your underarm. You will not be thinking at all. That's what chanting is all about. Sometimes I just use my name.

- **Visualisation**: This is a technique that I use at any time of day. Actually all of my techniques are functional solutions to all parts of your life, not just marathon training. Visualisation is akin to daydreaming or pretending. Call it what you like, visualisation is powerful. I have seen people transform their moods and motivation through this practice.

It helps to have a few pictures 'in the can' before you need them. For example, on a hot or muggy day, you may want to have previously developed a picture in your head about sitting in a lounge chair with your feet immersed in a nearby lake or pool while sipping an icy drink with a wet towel wrapped around the back of your neck.

Create your own mental pictures for situations that cover bad racing weather, physical aches, emotional slumps and more. Be prepared. Write them down. Practice them while lying in bed. Know your pictures so well that you can conjure them in a second.

- **Other mind tricks**: People know me for using every available tool imaginable to make marathon training and races easier and more fun. Here are a few other fun ideas you may want to try:
  - count the number of walkers vs runners
  - count how many people you overtake per km
  - look for someone interesting and try to keep up with him/her
  - count how many people are wearing a certain colour
  - think about the new clothes you're going to buy and how great you'll look in them
  - think about the next destination
  - think about the post-event party
  - repeat your name as a mantra
  - repeat positive affirmations for a specific distance then change the affirmation to another favorite.
  - use affirmations like "I am unstoppable" or "I am on fire!" or "PB (Personal Best), PB, PB!".

➤ *The mind is a powerful thing, use it! The marathon is a mental challenge as much as a physical one.*

8. NUTRITION & HYDRATION

Here's a list of everything you may need to make your marathon journey easier.

NUTRITION & HYDRATION

In the past, water, sports drinks and fruit were the mainstay of a marathon walker or runner. Not anymore. With the proliferation of new walkers and runners, manufacturers have developed new drinks, supplements and food items that are designed to speed the delivery of glycogen to our muscles.

As I explained earlier, the body uses either stored fat or glycogen as fuel when you're running or walking. When you are going slower, the body is using stored fat. As you go faster, the body uses more glycogen as fuel. Our bodies only store a certain amount of glycogen in our muscles, enough to fuel us approximately for 30 km. So supplementing our glycogen stores becomes very important for participating in marathons.

Energy gels

Energy gels are now commonly used as carbohydrate supplements. I find them quite effective in terms of boosting blood glucose and they're very portable as well.

Energy bars

Athletes love their energy bars; marathoners need them the most. In an effort to keep fueling our body's muscles and blood, we want to find enjoyable ways to do that.

There are so many different energy bars. I recommend you find the brand that delivers the most nutrition for the size and price and experiment with flavors and quantities as you train. For example; you may love peanut butter, but it may not agree with you while you're exerting energy.

Vitamins and supplements

Every marathoner has their own list of vitamins and supplements they think are mandatory, but these are the common ones:

- **Omega-3 fatty acid:** Lowers cholesterol, is an anti-inflammatory and a natural painkiller for sore muscles. *Foods: tuna and salmon*

- **Calcium:** Great for bones, repetitive motion. *Foods: milk, orange juice, tofu, broccoli, kale and spinach*

- **Iron**: Allows oxygen to be transferred to the muscles. Low levels instigate fatigue and colds. *Foods: red meat, lentils and broccoli*

- **Folic acid:** Keeps blood cells healthy, reduces possibility of anemia and heart disease. *Foods: grains, leafy greens, vegetables, lentils, cereals (e.g. oatmeal), citrus fruits*

- **Glucosamine:** A protein constituent in tendons, cartilage and ligaments; relieves joint pain and can also help repair injuries. *Foods: shrimp, lobster, crab*

- **Vitamin C:** An antioxidant, it protects the body from stress and pollution and strengthens immune systems. *Foods: oranges, kiwi, cranberries, tomatoes and strawberries*

- **Vitamin E:** Reported to protect us from the damage that can be caused by long distance running or walking. *Foods: almonds, wheat germ and fortified cereals*

- **Zinc:** Helps the immune system, interacts with enzymes and provides energy. Zinc is lost in perspiration, so it is important to replenish. *Foods: wheat germ, beef, poultry, pork, lamb and seafood*

Drinks

Different people require different amounts of liquid to hydrate, so you need to experiment to work out what is the correct amount for your long distance sessions. Besides dehydration, it's also important not to drink too much water when you are not thirsty as you could get hyponatremia or water intoxication.

Because the feeling of thirst only appears when you are already dehydrated, it is important not to skip drinks when you are not thirsty. So if you are not thirsty, you must still take a few sips at the hydration station and use the rest of the cup to wash your face or to cool your head. If you feel thirsty, you must grab two cups and drink both.

You can check your hydration levels by looking at the colour of your urine during or just after training. If you are well hydrated, your urine should be clear to pale yellow in colour. If it is yellow or dark yellow, you need to drink more during training.

- **Water:** There are so many varieties of water to drink – tap water, bottled water and so on. Take your pick. You may be using water bottles that are included with your belt or pack. No matter how you decide to carry them, remember the rule of thumb: 250ml (approximately one cup) of water roughly every 20 mins, but do not drink to excess (in case of hyponatremia).

- **Sports drinks:** Sports drinks are filled with electrolytes and carbohydrates, so I highly encourage taking a combination of water and sports drinks on all long distance routes. If you know the type of sports drink that will be provided during the event, give it a try during your training. Don't wait until the day of a race to try out a new drink.

- **Alcohol - none:** Need I say more? Alcohol is dehydrating and counter-productive to training. That is all you need to remember. If you are having an after-marathon party, limit yourself to one or two drinks.

Make your own

I can be a little fussy at times and don't like many store-purchased energy bars. They are often too sweet for my taste. They are also filled with preservatives. Making your own doesn't take long and they can be made in quantity and stored in the freezer. Since this is not a cookbook, I won't spend much time going into this.

I start with a base of: bananas, honey, oats, whole wheat flour, cinnamon, walnuts or slivered almonds, dried prunes or cranberries and a little vanilla. Then I add whatever else might work, such as: wheat germ, tahini and dried blueberries.

Do an Internet search for more recipes and detailed instructions. There are also recipes for making your own sports drink. I like to mix chia seeds and lemon juice in water. Remember to stick to recipes that use natural ingredients.

Nutrition for races

Just like hydration, nutrition can make or break the success of your race. Glycogen stored will be used up 30 km into the race so use that rule of thumb when planning your pre-marathon meals and snacks. I'll go into this more in future chapters, but here is some basic information.

- **Long runs:** Experiment during your training to determine what will keep you going. My rule of thumb is to eat carbohydrates every 90 minutes or so if you are a walker, so go from there. If you prefer to go by distance, eat every 10 km or so. Be generous in your planning so you have extra nourishment during your first few long runs. You'll soon know what works for your body and energy levels.

- **The week before:** Carbs will be a primary part of your diet during a lot of the training and pre-race periods. You will want to consume about 70% of your intake in carbs, preferably complex carbohydrates.

- **Three days before:** You can start carbo-loading, where 90% of your calories consumed will be carbs (read *Chapter 11: One Week Before* for more details on carbo-loading).

> ➢ *Be creative! It doesn't have to be just pasta, rice and sweet potatoes. Don't forget about oats, quinoa and couscous. Do not skip meals. Consuming a steady amount of calories prior to a marathon is all part of maintaining consistency in preparation and performance.*

- **The day before:** You are still in carbo-loading mode, so today you will indulge yourself in 90% of your calories from carbohydrates, double your water intake and rest. **Have your last big meal no less than 12 hours from the start of the race.** Only consume what you have been regularly eating up to the race; don't try new types of food. Avoid heavy foods such as red meat and cheese as they take a long time to digest.

- **The day itself:** Snack two hours ahead of the event and no big meals. Avoid heavy foods such as red meat and cheese as they take a long time to digest. Drink about half a litre of fluids two hours before the start. Then have another drink (one or two cups) in the last hour before the start.

- **During the marathon:** We've covered this earlier, but it is important to remember. **Every 90 minutes or so, replenish your carbohydrates. Every 20 minutes or so, replenish your fluids**.

- **After the marathon:** After the event, the priority is to replenish fluids. It's important to get electrolytes back in the body, so I'd usually drink approximately one litre of sports drink (slowly, over a period of 30 minutes or so). Don't eat immediately after the race, and when you do, carbohydrates and protein should be on your plate. My favourite is chocolate milk and chicken pasta soon after a marathon.

The temptation to reward yourself with junk food and soft drinks will be quite high after a marathon. If you're planning on continuing the life of a marathoner, don't give in to that sugar craving.

9. AVOIDING INJURIES

Don't let anyone tell you to expect injuries. They can be avoided with the right prep.

AVOIDING INJURIES

Running or walking a marathon is definitely a challenge, make no mistake. If you aren't prepared, you could injure yourself quickly and be forced to opt out of the race.

With the correct training regime, most marathoners will be able to avoid injuries. My **30/30 Method** is designed for injury prevention, conserving energy and maintaining speed. Adding strength and cross-training will add to increased stamina and fewer possibilities of injuries.

If you feel an injury coming on, don't ignore it. Increase your Slow walking period straightaway.

Blisters are your enemy

It's hard to finish a marathon without at least a few blisters. Because of training, your feet no longer have the soft pads they use to have. You've already bought the best shoes and socks for your feet, right? And, practised which creams or lubricants work best on your feet?

You will need to practise draining and covering your blisters, so that they can heal quickly.

Avoiding and treating problems

- **Muscle strain:** Muscle strain can come in the form of a pulled hamstring or calf muscle. In either case, it's not very comfortable. To treat strains and sprains use ice, compression, elevation and rest.

- **Tendon pain:** Tendon pain is usually caused by overuse and 'over-pronating', which is excessive rotation of the foot. Rest is usually the best answer for tendon pain. If you want to continue to train, consider using a stationary bike for short periods.

- **Runner's knee:** Runner's knee is the most common injury for runners and the pain is found where the kneecap meets the thigh bone. This is usually due to weak quadriceps and tight hamstrings. Strengthening these muscles could help avoid this injury.

  If your foot strike tends to over/under-pronate, the kneecap undergoes a sideways pressure, also creating injuries. Wearing motion-control shoes or walking on a smoother and soft-ground course can help.

- **Sore back:** A common ailment for marathoners, this is usually caused by weak abdomen muscles, which support the back. A sore back almost always mean the core needs strengthening. While walking, do concentrate on good posture.

- **Swollen hands:** Swollen hands and toes are a frequent occurrence after a marathon. Possible reasons for this are extreme loss of electrolytes or too much salt in the diet or over-hydration. Once you identify the cause, the solution is easy. Replenish electrolytes, use less salt or drink less water, depending on the issue.

➢ *To reduce swollen hands during a long walk/run, shake your hands violently as if you are flicking water off them. Your hands will feel better after a minute.*

- **Chafing:** Protect areas that are prone to chafing with lubricant or Vaseline.

- **Side stitch:** Getting a side stitch is no fun and can be debilitating. It's that sharp pain in your side that happens unexpectedly. There are several schools of thought as to why it happens, but the thing you need to know is how to make it go away quickly. First off, slow down to a slow walk. Then start belly breathing with long inhalations that result in a 'grunt' exhale. Massaging the stitch area gently may also help.

- **Shin splints:** Pain in the front of your lower leg, directly over the shinbone, or on the inner/outer sides, is known as shin splints. Over-pronation and overuse are the primary causes of shin splints, though there are other possibilities, such as stress fractures. The best treatment is ice, elevation, rest and, possibly, orthotics. If it persists, see a doctor.

- **Plantar fasciitis:** Heel pain is the best way to explain plantar fasciitis. Plantar fasciitis is usually the result of overuse. Excessive pronation is another cause, as is arthritis. The best cure is to stay off your feet for a while and give them a break. If it persists, see a doctor.

- **ITBS (Iliotibial Band Syndrome)**: ITBS affects many runners, causing lateral knee pain. The band runs up the outer side of the knee, and extends to the pelvis. It's a part of the body that helps stabilise the knees when walking or running. If you see swelling or feel pain above the knee area, it may be ITBS. Treatment for ITBS is rest, ice, compression and elevation.

- **Muscle cramps:** Dehydration and salt depletion are the primary causes of muscle cramps. This is not something to mess with if you experience it during a race. Stop and massage the affected muscle, consume a sports drink and salt tablet and continue as soon as you can, by walking slowly until the affected muscle recovers.

➤ *Remember to carry salt tablets during marathons to combat cramps.*

- **Heatstroke:** Doing a marathon in hot weather can be hazardous to anyone's health and needs to be handled with care. Overheating results when the body can't adequately cool itself by sweating. To combat this dangerous condition make sure you have trained in the same level of heat and humidity as your marathon event.

  Also, drink about 250 ml (one cup) of water or sports drink every 20 minutes or so. If you find yourself heat-exhausted and your urine is dark yellow in colour, rest under shade and consider opting out of the race. If you continue, you could experience heatstroke, which is most definitely an emergency condition.

- **Sunburn:** To start with, dress smart. A hat with a wide brim is a necessity in locations that have full sun beating down during the entire race. Do apply sunscreen and lip balm frequently. Also, consider your clothing. Lightweight materials that cover most of your bare skin might keep you cooler and avoid sunburn more easily.

- **Dehydration:** Record your hydration intake before, during and after your training in your logbook. By the time you embark on your first marathon you will already know your water replenishment needs. Avoiding dehydration should be easy. Follow the 250 ml (one cup) of fluids every 20 minutes guideline (or slightly more in locations that are warmer).

  If you start feeling irritable or dizzy, or experience any back pain or headache, do slow down and drink a cup or two of sports drink. If possible, check the colour of your urine. If it is yellow or dark yellow in colour, you need to drink urgently.

- **Over-hydration:** Most people don't realise that it is possible to over hydrate. Believe it or not, if you drink too much, you can get nausea, cramps, bloating and swollen glands. It can be as dangerous as being dehydrated. So avoid drinking too much at every drink station if you don't feel thirsty.

> ### FINAL TIPS FOR AVOIDING INJURIES

- Avoid over/under-pronation by using the right shoes and, if necessary, customised orthotics.

- Strengthen your weaker muscles with cross-training.

- Prepare properly for weather conditions.

- Go slower when going up and down slopes.

- Practice on similar terrains and slopes that you will find on the marathon course.

10. TAPERING

Just when you may think you should increase your training, it's time to slow down.

TAPERING

Tapering is exactly what it sounds like: tapering off from training before a big race. Many beginner marathoners baulk at the thought of tapering, as they think it might be counterproductive. It is actually just the opposite.

Tapering is an essential part of marathon training. A review of 50 studies on tapering published in the journal, *Medicine & Science in Sports & Exercise*, showed that the body repairs itself during the tapering period. Those who tapered in these studies improved their marathon times by five to 10 minutes.

Tapering is a method that works to regain your optimal energy and fitness for a race. So too short a taper might leave you tired on race day and too long a taper might leave you out of shape. Finding the right balance is the key to walking your best race.

For beginners, I recommend a three-week tapering schedule before the marathon event. More experienced marathoners who do marathons frequently can shorten this tapering period to two weeks if they want to.

Tapering in the Training Plans

If you have been using the **Beginner 1, 2 or 3 training plans**, the tapering will look as follows.

Three weeks before the marathon	One week before
• Two x 30 minute sessions • Long distance session of 32 km (20 miles); this is the maximum distance in these training plans	• Two x 30 minute sessions • Long distance session of 12 km (7.5 miles)
Tapering starts ...	**Marathon week** • Two x 30 minute sessions
Two weeks before • Two x 30 minute sessions • Long distance session of 20 km (12.4 miles)	**Marathon!**

For those on the **Intermediate and Advanced training plans,** the tapering is as follows.

Three weeks before the marathon	• Long distance session of 12 km (7.5 miles)
• Two x 30 minute sessions • Long distance session of 34 km; these are the maximum distances in these training plans	• One cross-training session • One strength training session • Start fueling up on carbs • Hydrate with water and sports drinks
Tapering starts ...	**Marathon week** • Two x 30 minute sessions
Two weeks before • Two x 30 minute sessions • Long distance session of 20 km (12.4 miles)	**Day before** Short session for 20 minutes (optional)
One week before • Two x 30 minute sessions	**Marathon!**

➢ *Decrease the distance but maintain the intensity of your training when tapering.*

Eat normally

One thing that you must not do is to eat less during the tapering period. Please continue to eat normal amounts as this will increase the glycogen stores and red blood cells in your body. By the time of the marathon event, your body will be fully fueled up.

Be prepared for sluggishness

Many people will feel slightly sluggish during the taper. Some will even feel cranky due to the reduced amount of training. Many will complain that they are putting on a little weight.

This is normal. Don't panic and conclude that your fitness level is dropping. Stick to the tapering, and you will be supercharged when marathon day comes.

Use tapering time to mentally rehearse the marathon

This is a good time to mentally prepare. Imagine how your marathon could go wrong and mentally rehearse how you would address the issue. For example:
- What would you do if you developed a stitch?
- What would you do if it rained heavily and your socks got soaked?
- What would you do if you developed a blister?

Short session the day before the marathon

In my intermediate and advanced training plans, I recommend doing a 20-minute training session the day before the marathon. This will keep the blood pumping through your legs. This 20-minute session is optional for beginners.

Final Tips

- You don't want to catch a cold one week before your marathon. As far as possible, try to keep away from crowds and friends who are having a cold.

- Don't do anything tiring, such as rock climbing or playing a long game of tennis.

- Sleep as much as you can during the week before the marathon.

11. ONE WEEK BEFORE

It's time to relax, reflect and follow a plan that will enhance your experience.

ONE WEEK BEFORE

As with any sport, there are different schools of thought on how to best prepare for a marathon. If you're like most marathoners, you'll start to feel excited, 'antsy' and uncertain.

If you're traveling for the race, the experience can be a bit more intense. Let's go through a sample week and then I'll give you the tips that have helped me each and every time. In this chapter, I will include examples for those who have been using **Beginner 1, 2 and 3 training plans**.

5 days before the marathon
- 30-minute training session, as scheduled in the training plan.
- Study the course map and rehearse and visualise your perfect marathon day.
- Wake up and eat the same as you will do on the morning of the race. Train at the same time you will start on race day.
- Kick up the hydration levels for the rest of the week.

4 days before the marathon
- Stick with the wake, eat, train, hydrate pattern established yesterday.
- Cross-train with an activity that will support your endurance and strength; low-impact is best.
- Eat at the same dinner time you plan to eat the evening before the marathon.

3 days before the marathon
- Rest today.
- Start to carbo-load with mostly complex carbohydrates, e.g. whole grains.

2 days before the marathon
- 30-minute training session, as scheduled in the training plan.
- Study the course map again. Rehearse and visualise your perfect marathon day during your 30 minute session.
- Afterwards, take a warm shower or bath, to increase blood circulation. Increase your salt intake slightly, but don't overdo it. Follow the same routine started on '5 days before the marathon' with sleeping, eating and training. For carbo-loading, switch to simple carbs, e.g. pasta, white bread and potatoes.

1 day before the marathon
- You might be feeling sluggish due to the reduced volume of training this week, but that is normal. You can add a light 20-minute workout, but keep the intense portions to bursts of 1-2 minutes.
- Today is also the day to pack your gear and bags.
- Increase your salt intake slightly, but don't overdo it.
- Continue with the simple carbs. Eat a big plate of pasta. Avoid cream sauces and dairy products. Your last big meal should be 12 hours before the start of your marathon.

Sleep

Sleep is a 'tool of the trade', meaning it is essential if you want to have a pleasant marathon experience. Not everyone requires the same amount, but 8 hours a night seems to be the ideal. The importance of bringing up the topic of sleep is to remind everyone to make a concerted effort to get their ideal amount of sleep all week prior to the marathon.

Since you may have had to practise getting up early a few times this week, maximise your sleep time by going to bed earlier.

Check the course map

Checking your marathon routes makes it easier to know what to expect. Every race provides a course map and if you haven't already studied it in depth, which I hope you have, this week is the time to go through it in great detail.

Study the **course map** to familiarise yourself with:

- the overall course
- hydration stops
- toilets
- medical areas
- start and finish lines
- landmarks
- terrain (check out the uphill portions).

If you are going to do the '4 x 10 Breakdown', you will need to check out the landmarks located around the 2 km, 12 km, 22 km and 32 km marks.

If you're going to a new destination for the event, and haven't had a chance to study the terrain, download an app, such as Google Earth, or watch footage of previous marathons held there to see the terrain up close. Some course maps now have online interactive versions, which will give you pertinent information from the start to the finish line.

Work out the logistics

Once you've closely reviewed the course, it's time to work out the logistics. Locate the hotel, parking, public transport, nearby restaurants, toilets, the start and finish lines. Work out how you'll get to and from each place.

If you're staying at a hotel, you will want to make sure the food you want to consume is readily available.

You'll want to get to the destination at least a day in advance in order to pick up your race kit, and also to investigate anything that couldn't be researched on the Internet or phone. As stated above, figure out how you will get to the start line, and where to meet your family/friends when you finish. Have a back-up plan, in the event you get injured and can't finish.

Checklist: marathon day supplies

Buy your final supplies and pack your bag in the week prior to the marathon. To get you started, here's a checklist of basic things to consider.

☐ Blister kit	☐ Race number and timing
☐ Energy bars, food, snacks	chip (if applicable)
☐ Gloves (if cold)	☐ Running jacket (if cold)
☐ Hat or visor	☐ Salt tablets
☐ Lubricant	☐ Shoes & Socks
☐ Post-marathon change of	☐ Sports bra
clothes (especially if	☐ Sunglasses
there's no post–race top)	☐ Sunscreen
☐ Running belt, armband or	☐ Toilet paper
fanny pack	☐ Travel documents
☐ Prescriptions, vitamins,	(passport, plane tickets,
supplements	hotel booking
☐ Race gear (shorts, t-shirt /	confirmation, etc)
sleeveless top and long	☐ Watch (GPS)
sleeved top)	☐ Water bottles
	☐ Water or sports drinks

Carbo-loading

Carbo-loading is important because carbs are the primary source of fuel for the marathon. Noodles, potatoes, rice and other high-carbohydrate foods are going to give you the fuel to get through 'The Wall'. Going the distance requires a lot of fuel and as I mentioned in earlier chapters, your muscles only store enough to last about 30 km, depending on variables like speed and body mass.

My rule of thumb is to start carbo-loading about three days before the race. About 90% of your calories should come from carbs during those last three days.

Although many fruits are high in carbs, they should not be the only choice due to possible stomach reactions because of their high fibre content. High-fat foods are also not a wise choice as they take longer to digest.

During carbo-loading, you need to include two or three of these carbs in every meal: bread, rice, noodles, pasta, potatoes, cereal and fruit. Check out the following sample carbo-loading menu.

Sample carbo-loading menu

MEAL 1 (breakfast)
Rice, oats or quinoa with blueberry jam
Banana
Orange or tomato juice
Multigrain toast

MEAL 2 (morning snack)
Granola
Prunes
Yoghurt, plain
Bagel

MEAL 3 (lunch)
Noodles with sauce
Bread with olive oil
Cookies

MEAL 4 (afternoon snack)
Energy bar
Potato and cauliflower soup
Bread with olive oil

MEAL 5 (dinner)
Lasagna with marinara sauce
Brussel sprouts, roasted
French bread with olive oil and minced garlic

MEAL 6 (night snack)
Toasted muffin and jam
Sports drink

12. ONE DAY BEFORE

You are ready! Tomorrow is the day you've been planning for, and now it's time to get excited.

ONE DAY BEFORE

There are so many things to remember before starting your marathon. You might be a little nervous and excited. By now, you should feel great about your training. If you've followed my training plans, you should be ready and raring to go. You have arrived. Tomorrow is the big day!

Before you start losing focus, let's go over the *'Day before Checklist'* so you can be fully prepared.

DAY BEFORE CHECKLIST

Pack race bag and running belt
See the *'Checklist: marathon day supplies'* in Chapter 11 for your race bag. I would add the following for the running belt:
- money for taxi and snacks after the race
- train or bus travel card
- your house/car keys
- mobile phone
- music player and earphones (if allowed)

Hydrate: We've discussed dehydration and over-hydration, so you know the dangers of both. The day before the big day, be sure to drink water throughout the day and add in a sports drink or two for the electrolytes. No alcohol.

Eat well: By now you are prepared and knowledgeable about loading up on carbohydrates beginning a couple days ago. Today you should eat 90% of your calories in carbs. That doesn't mean over-eating, just eating enough to fuel those muscles.

Short training session

- **Beginning marathoners:** This is your day to relax!

- **Intermediate and advanced marathoners:** You know you want it, so go ahead, go for a short training session to release any anxiety and build some last-minute confidence. The session shouldn't last more than 20 minutes. Don't overdo it. Conserve your energy. During the session, imagine running through the marathon's finish line.

Miscellaneous tasks

You should also do the following:

- Plan how to travel to the event. Aim to arrive one hour before the start of the race. If you're driving, add some time to allow for parking.

- Memorise the locations of the bag deposit area, the toilets, the starting line and the finish line.

- Pin your race bib or number to your top (you'll need four safety pins to do it, unless you like your race bib to flap in the wind).

- Some timing chips need to be tied to your shoes. After tying the chip, put on your shoes to check that the chip is not tied too tightly and possibly interfering with your blood circulation.

- Fill up a water bottle with your drink of choice. You will be discarding this bottle before the start of the race.

- Pack your snacks into a small zip lock bag

- Shake out any sand or gravel from your shoes.

- Today is the day to shave areas of your body that have experienced chafing during training.

- Today is also the day to trim your toenails. Do not cut too close, or bleeding could occur on race day.

- Very important: Charge your GPS watch, mobile phone, and music player. If you're bringing a battery pack, charge that too.

Two alarm clocks

I probably don't need to explain the thought behind the two alarm clock rule. In case you have trouble sleeping the night before the marathon, you are going to want to have a backup plan to ensure you wake up on time.

Welcome to my simple backup plan: **TWO ALARM CLOCKS**. Battery operated is my preference, in the event the electricity temporarily goes out overnight. I have two mobile phones, and I set alarms on both of them.

What time should you set the alarm? Here's how to figure it out: I recommend you give yourself at least 45 minutes to get ready after waking up. And let's assume you need 1 hour (including walking and parking) to get to the race venue. And I strongly recommend that you arrive at the race venue 1 hour before the start time. So you should set your alarm clock 2 hours 45 minutes (45 min + 1 hour + 1 hour) before the start of the marathon.

Final Tip

You will probably find it hard to sleep the night before the marathon. Don't worry too much about it. If you have been tapering properly, your body will be rested enough to handle a little lack of sleep. Good night, and good luck for your marathon!

13. MARATHON DAY

Today is the big day, and you are ready for it — enjoy the experience!

MARATHON DAY – today is the day!

What to do first?

Start by staying calm and being thankful you got this far. You got up on time and are feeling great! What a good start. I've laid out a step-by-step 'order of proceedings' for how this day will best play out. Make a few custom changes, but try to stick with it for your first few marathons.

MORNING
- Wake up and drink 500-750ml (2-3 cups) of water
- Eat a light breakfast
- Go to the toilet (empty your bowels)
- Apply Vaseline or lubricant before leaving the house
- Get there early (one hour before the start of the race)
- Continue drinking until one hour before the start of the race
- Go to the toilet 20 minutes before the start of the race (go earlier if the queues are long). Go twice if there is time.
- Warm up 10 minutes before the start of the race

WHAT TO EAT AND DRINK (a typical example)
- **One hour before:** Water and energy bar. To avoid toilet breaks during the marathon, don't drink too much after this.
- **10 minutes before:** handful of almonds
- **16 km:** energy gel*
- **21 km:** energy gel
- **27 km:** energy gel, maybe a salt tablet as well
- **32 km:** banana (usually provided by organisers)
- **38 km:** energy gel

* Instead of energy gel, I often substitute jelly beans, chocolate or glucose tablets as snacks

Marathon strategies and tactics

Not all marathons are the same, so you will want to plan your tactics in advance for each event. Fortunately, you have trained and are prepared for anything. A couple of things are different on the day of the marathon that are worth noting.

Pacing

A common mistake made by beginners is to start out fast while you're stronger. This is a fallacy. The more energy you expend in the beginning, the less you can muster up in the last half.

Marathons are about doing the last half well. Read the previous sentence again. Conserve your energy.

You have paced yourself at a specific speed for a reason, so today is not the day to make changes. Endurance pacing is a smart strategy. It's easy to spot a beginner when I see runners who sprint out of the gate.

Instead, let's use the **'4 x 10 Breakdown'** to guide your strategy.

- **The first 2 km** are a warm up. So take it easy and ignore the fact that most people will be overtaking you at this stage. You will be about 15 to 30 seconds per kilometre slower than your target pace.

- After the warm up stage, speed up to target pace for **the next 10 km.** This leg will seem easy but you must fight the temptation to speed up. Stick to your target pace.

- **The second 10 km leg** will also seem quite easy. Usually endorphins are kicking in and you might feel invincible. Once again, do not try to speed up and exceed your target pace at this stage.

- **The third 10 km leg** will probably be the most challenging. Fatigue will have set in and you will start to doubt yourself. This is the time to increase your Slow Walks and eat lots of snacks/gels. Be aware that you could hit 'The Wall' at the end of this stage.

- **The final 10 km** will depend on how well you trained. If you skipped important parts of your training plan, this last 10 km will be torturous. You will probably be vowing to yourself never to do a marathon again. (I've made this vow at least three or four times!) But if you trained well, the last 10 km is usually a bit easier than the third 10 km.

  Enthusiastic support from the crowds and the thought of finishing will keep your spirits up. If things get really bad, just do Slow Walks until you feel better. If possible, save a last burst of energy to run the last 500 metres.

Hydration

You now know that hydration is one of the top ingredients for doing a successful marathon. You need to stay hydrated during the entire race without becoming dehydrated or over-hydrated. If you are not thirsty at the hydration station, just take a sip and douse your head with the rest of the water. If you are thirsty, grab two cups and drink both.

Avoid the temptation to stand still while drinking at the hydration station! Practise walking and drinking at the same time and you will save a few valuable minutes in your marathon time.

Food

The food goal is to make sure you continue to feed carbs into the body so that the glycogen supply is maintained. I have outlined it above and will simply stress it here: **Don't let your fuel deplete!** Eat something every 90 minutes or so.

Low blood sugar

Snack, snack, snack – low blood sugar can be cured instantly by eating something with sugar in it. I usually carry a small ziplock bag of jelly beans and chocolate-coated peanuts for this purpose. If you are a diabetic, bring supplies for injections, or glucose tablets - whichever works for your specific condition.

Toilet breaks

You hope you won't need to make toilet stops, but you might as well be prepared. Each toilet break will delay you by a few minutes, so try to be quick and efficient. If you see a long queue at the toilets, consider taking another 20 minutes to walk to the next toilet, as queues waste valuable time. This is where it helps to have done your homework so you know where the toilets are located on the route.

In all my marathons, I have usually needed to make at least one toilet break.

Heat

Heat affects marathoners considerably. On hot days, you must go slower, for example, by increasing the ratio of Slow Walks. On a hot day, expect to add about 20 minutes to your target marathon time, or about 30 seconds slower per kilometre.

Drink more at every station, and pour water on your head regularly. Don't wear a hat, use a visor instead. Wear a sleeveless top if you have one.

Fatigue

Experiencing extreme fatigue while doing a marathon is something I've often experienced and seen in other marathoners. Often it is caused by something you neglected in your training plan or it could also be the weather. The main thing is that you can quickly recover if you increase the Slow Walk component of your walking strategy.

For example, if your Fast Walk - Slow Walk ratio is 30/30 then when fatigue hits, move into a 15/45 ratio. Also, take shorter strides. You should regain your energy soon after.

In addition, consider dropping to a Slow Walk during any uphill slopes to avoid additional fatigue.

The Wall

I'm sure you've heard horror stories of runners hitting 'The Wall'. Some runners describe this sensation as an invisible force that they come up against during a marathon.

What really happens is that you've run out of glycogen – the fuel needed to keep you going. Consider this: If you're burning an average of 75 calories per km, by the time you reach the finish line you've burned over 3100 calories, which is more than an entire day's nutrition needs for most people.

- **How it feels:** Hitting 'The Wall' is a feeling of total exhaustion. Your legs will feel heavy. There's a loss of focus and an uncertainty about why you are continuing.

- **Hitting 'The Wall' is avoidable:** Since you know the winning formula includes keeping the body burning both fat and glycogen, you can avoid this issue.

Remember: When you go at a slower pace, you burn mostly fat. As you increase speed, the body uses mostly glycogen as fuel. When the glycogen is depleted, the body reverts back to burning fat as fuel. We all have enough body fat to fuel us through many marathons, but since fat requires aerobic activity to burn you have to slow down a little in order for the fat to be used.

The goal is to approach the marathon properly trained, so you will be less winded and have available oxygen when you need it. That, plus eating carbohydrates as recommended, will keep you on track and using both fat and glycogen.

➤ *If you hit 'The Wall', increase your Slow Walk component so that the Fast Walk - Slow Walk ratio is 15/45.*

Tips for tackling common mid-race issues

- **If you get cramps:** Pull over and massage the cramp until it is entirely gone. Eat a salt tablet.

- **If you are injured:** If it's a mild injury, you may be able to continue walking after a bit of a rest and massage. If the pain persists, signal for help. Do not continue to race and make the problem worse. Don't worry: there is always another marathon.

- **If you see someone else injured:** Signal someone on the side of the course or use your mobile phone to call emergency services. If the person is unconscious or incoherent, don't leave them stranded by the side of the road. The race is important, but not more important than another person's safety.

- **If you need something:** Signal to a race official if it is urgent. Or always carry your mobile phone with you during the marathon.

The Finish Line

The last few kilometres may be torturous, but remember the pain will be temporary. Give everything you've got in the last 500 metres and go as fast as you can. Let the spectators' cheers push you on. Give a smile to the official photographers as you cross the finish line. Congratulations!

14. AFTER THE EVENT

*After all your hard work and train-
ing, you made it! And, you're now a
marathoner — congratulations!*

AFTER THE EVENT

First 10 minutes after

You can expect a few emotional moments after you make it through the finish line. It's hard to know in advance just how you will feel.

Many marathoners are starving and want nothing more than to eat, while others feel like throwing up. Considering the last few hours have affected every part of your body, mind and spirit you should allow yourself to experience anything.

Obviously, cooling down is a priority and highly recommended before eating anything. Personally, I suggest you walk around a little and get some sugar into your body, such as a glucose tablet, energy gel or even sugary gum.

Hydrate

Water is good, while a sports drink will help you recover and rehydrate even faster. It's your choice. Any way you look at it, the first 10 minutes after the finish line can be bad for health if you don't rehydrate immediately.

Check your GPS watch

Now is the perfect time to check your time and other statistics that you have been measuring during the entire training period.

Get your medal, t-shirt and goodie bag

Now is a great time to go over to the finish line tables and collect your goodies. You've earned them. The usual swag will be some sort of medal, a promotional t-shirt that proves you completed the marathon and a gift bag comprising sponsors' freebies, coupons and the like.

No stretching

From experience, I advise waiting for a few hours before stretching. Your body is stiff and needs to return to normalcy in its own time. Forcing it to stretch before the muscles and ligaments have a chance to bounce back can cause injuries, cramping and other unnecessary problems.

First hour after the race

Eat

Now you can eat and be sure you're not going to get sick. After the first 10 minutes, if you are somewhat cooled down, hunger may set in.

This is a good time to consume as much protein and carbs that you can ingest comfortably. I don't mean stuff yourself. I mean eating intelligently to help the body regain its strength.

Ice bath

Sounds cold, doesn't it? An ice bath can reduce muscle soreness after any exercise, but especially after a marathon. To do an ice bath, you need to get home or to your hotel room as soon as possible and add ice to a bathtub of water. Submerge your legs and feet in the ice bath for about 10 minutes.

If you are unable to get to a bathtub within an hour, douse a towel or t-shirt in icy water and work it on all of the sore parts of your body for about 10 minutes or so. Inflammation in the muscles, tendons and ligaments will be reduced.

Massage

Within the hour after finishing your race, a short massage will feel great. A full body massage is best done a little later in the day. In the meantime, go ahead and massage those sore body parts. In fact, grab a fellow marathoner and help each other.

Taking care of your muscles and achy joints within the first hour will do wonders in terms of reducing aches and pains later. Many marathons even have massage tents set up at the finish line to reward weary participants – so look out for those and enjoy!

Fix any blisters

You may be lucky enough to complete a full marathon without experiencing blisters. However, quite a number of us will experience blisters at some point or another in the race.

Taking care of any blisters as soon as you're able will help them heal faster. Go to the medical tent, if there is one, or prepare a blister kit ahead of time.

The blister kit should contain:
- alcohol wipes, to clean the blister area
- a safety pin, to pierce the blister
- small scissors, to cut away the skin
- antiseptic cream
- bandaids of various sizes.

3-6 hours after the race

Walk some more, just a little

Your body is now starting to find its centre. This is a good time to move around more, go for a slow walk or a shakeout run. It will keep your limbs loose and keep you from being sore.

Try to resist the temptation to sleep the whole afternoon! I've done this once, and woke up feeling very sore.

Stretch

After you loosen up with a little walk or run, it's a perfect time to stretch. Move through your normal stretching routine slowly and deliberately.

Concentrate on elongating and relaxing your muscle groups while eliminating aches and pains.

Celebrate!

It's time to pamper, heal, reflect, rejuvenate and celebrate. Every cell in your body wants and deserves this time. What better way to end this day than to celebrate with your friends and family.

Congratulations, you did it!

15. POST MARATHON FORTNIGHT

Now it's time to re-live your marathon success and take extra care of yourself—you deserve it!

POST MARATHON FORTNIGHT

Delayed onset muscle soreness

You may or may not experience muscle soreness a couple of days after the marathon. It depends on the individual's body. If you have followed the training regime, the preparation, the tapering and the after-race advice, chances are you are feeling pretty good about now.

However, if you are still feeling a little sore and damaged, then pamper yourself even more. Massages and baths will go a long way. You just ran a marathon and deserve to honour every ache and pain that came as part of the package. Smile and be proud at your achievement.

Rest for a week

For beginners, it can take as long as a week for your body to feel completely repaired. After all the training, it might surprise you that it can take a while.

Some marathoners might recommend getting 'back on the horse' and getting out there again, but I feel it is an individual choice. If you're going to end up going out there and feeling lifeless, grumbling through an easy jog, then don't do it.

So I recommend one week of rest after the marathon. If you feel you really need to start training again, take at least two days off for some rest and relaxation.

Two weeks of rest is also okay if you start doing some cross-training in the second week, e.g. 30 minutes of swimming or cycling or yoga. **Resting for more than two weeks is not recommended if you want to maintain your fitness.**

Evaluate your marathon performance

When you are ready, compare your race statistics against your training notes. How do you feel? Did your strengths carry you through? Were your weaknesses heightened or lessened during the race?

How did you do versus your expectations? If you performed a little less efficiently than you expected, don't be disappointed. Completing a marathon is like putting on a live performance at the Sydney Opera House. Not every performance can be the same, no matter how frequently you train and practice. Real life plays a role and should be taken into consideration.

Specific questions you should ask
- Were your marathon goals realistic, given your level of fitness?
- How effective was your training plan?
- What problems did you face during the marathon and how did you adjust for them?
- When did you start to slow down in terms of speed?
- How comparable were your times for the first half and second half of the marathon?
- When did you start to peak in terms of heart rate?
- When did you have to depart from your Fast Walk – Slow Walk plan?
- How closely did you follow your nutrition and hydration strategy?

You may have outperformed your expectations, and that is amazing. Either way, reviewing your statistics is not intended to be a tool for chastising yourself. It just helps you to get a handle on the next steps.

Post-marathon blues

For some marathoners, life after a marathon can often feel like an anticlimax. This feeling is normal. After training so hard for so long, it is easy to feel that there is a 'void' in one's life.

My advice is to take a break from marathons and catch up with friends and family. In fact, I took a one year break after my first marathon. But eventually I went back to doing marathons again because I missed the challenging training process needed to prepare for a marathon.

Choose your next marathon

So if you are not facing post-marathon blues, now would be a perfect time to start thinking about your next marathon. Where will you go? How will it be different? How soon can you handle another?

Go ahead and plan one or more and then start your reverse taper. The reverse tapering will help you regain spent energy and renew your enthusiasm for the sport. Even if you have another marathon coming up, it's important to take the necessary break.

Reverse taper

Recovering from a marathon even more quickly is possible with a reverse taper. It will help you to build up your strength, determination and spirit all over again. It will remind you how much you love this sport and why you want to stick with it.

The training plans in *Chapter 6* have all been designed with a reverse taper in mind. To do a reverse taper, simply rest for one week after your last marathon, then start with Week 1 of a training plan that is relevant to you. Try not to rest more than three weeks after your last marathon, as your fitness will start to drop rapidly.

If you are unsure when your next marathon will be, rest one week then repeat the three-week cycle in *Training Plan 6* until you have confirmed the date of your next marathon.

16. THE MARATHON LIFESTYLE

If the marathon experience leaves you wanting more, why not consider adopting a marathon lifestyle?

THE MARATHON LIFESTYLE

A marathon lifestyle can be emotionally, physically, and, for some, even spiritually, fulfilling.

While most marathoners get hooked on the whole package, not just the race, living the marathon lifestyle is something you can embrace with as much depth as you wish.

If you are ready for more, then you've come to the right place. Here are a few strategies to get your started.

Living the Marathon Lifestyle involves:
- dedication to regular exercise
- dedication to healthy nutrition
- celebration of body, mind and spirit
- commitment to training and continuous, gradual improvement
- gaining more knowledge (and confidence) about marathons and your body
- passing on your knowledge and advice to marathon 'newbies'.

Do several local marathons a year

The marathon lifestyle involves signing up for marathons and other races throughout the year. Spread them out to give yourself time to taper and reverse taper.

Take a marathon holiday

Combining a trip with a marathon will provide an incredible vacation. Consider inviting family or friends to join you, and remember to plan enough days to accommodate any time changes or jet lag and recuperation time at the end.

Even if the time difference isn't enough to give you jetlag, arrive a few days early to get accustomed to the weather, location and to discover nearby conveniences. You'll need to find a store where you can buy water and other last minute items you might want.

Luckily many marathon routes are planned in busy metropolitan areas. Book a hotel near the sites you may want to see in the days following the race.

According to *Forbes Magazine*, the **Top 10 Marathons in the world** worth traveling for are:
- Napa Valley Marathon, California, USA
- Paris Marathon, Paris, France
- Boston Marathon, Boston, USA
- Virgin London Marathon, London, United Kingdom
- Big Sur International Marathon, California, USA
- Vancouver Marathon, Vancouver, Canada
- Mont St-Michel Bay Marathon, Mont St-Michel, France
- The Great Wall Marathon, Tianjin, China
- The Big Five Marathon, Limpopo Province, South Africa
- Athens Classic Marathon, Athens, Greece

Do your own personal marathon

There's nothing stopping you from creating your own 42 km route near where you live. Personally I like to go along rivers or beaches. Using my GPS watch as a guide, I would go 21.1 km one way, then U-turn back to the beginning, making it a full 42.2 km marathon. Just remember to:

- bring enough water (minimum 1 litre)
- bring enough snacks
- let others know the route you are taking
- bring a mobile phone and cash for emergencies
- choose a safe and well-trodden route, and
- don't do this at night or in unsuitable weather.

Maintenance plan for in-between marathons

As mentioned earlier, embracing the marathon lifestyle means doing several marathons a year. This means you need to have shorter training plans between your marathons to maintain your fitness. See Training Plan 6, *Chapter 6*, for three different variations of a maintenance training plan.

One way to find the motivation to walk as much as possible is to install apps like Moves or Noom Walk Pedometer on your smartphone. These free apps track how many steps you take in a day, 24/7. I usually take 7000 steps on an average day. On marathon days, I log nearly 60,000 steps.

Set a long-term goal

Having a goal gives a marathoner something to aspire to. Aiming to complete 100 marathons or a marathon in every country are common goals. Such goals will keep you going without having any moments of wishy-washy thinking.

If you don't set a marathon goal, you will find yourself waffling about when, where and how many marathons to do in the future.

Again, planning is the best way to stay inspired and in the game. If you do five or six marathons a year, which is a reasonable target, you can hit 100 marathons in less than 20 years. Seeing how people in their 80s are still doing marathons, you could start doing marathons in your 60s and still achieve 100 marathons within your lifetime!

If you do complete 100 marathons, you can join a '100 Marathon Club'. Two well-known clubs are in the UK (www.100marathonclub.org.uk) and North America (100marathonclub.us). There are many such clubs around the world, including in Australia, Germany, Ireland, The Netherlands and Russia.

Members of the 100 Marathon Club

Roger Biggs has done more than 800 marathons (800 at time of publication) and was the chairman of the UK 100 Marathon Club. Roger is an inspiration. His first marathon was the inaugural Stevenage Marathon in 1984, and he has not looked back.

Bob and Lenore Dolphin have an amazing track record. Bob ran his first marathon when he was 51 and his 500th at the age of 82. Bob and Lenore have been running together since 1994, and founded the North American 100 Club to give marathoners an admirable milestone to aspire to.

Brenton Floyd has done more than 300 races to date (at least 367 by December 2013). He is well-known for having completed 300 marathons by the time he turned 21 years of age.

Some inspiring marathoners

- **Fauja Singh (1911-present):** Sometimes called the Running Baba, Fauja is the oldest person to complete a marathon. In 2011, he was 100 years old when he finished the Toronto Waterfront Marathon in eight hours and 11 minutes. In July 2012, Fauja was a torchbearer for the London 2012 Olympic Games. His best time was in the London Marathon, which he finished in six hours and two minutes, at the age of 91.

- **Kathrine Switzer (1947-present):** Kathrine is the first woman to run the previously all-male Boston Marathon. She evaded the race director's efforts to drag her out of the race and managed to complete the event. She has become an important feminist figure and author.

- **Dick Hoyt (1940-present) and Rick Hoyt (1962-present):** This father and son team has finished more than 1000 races of all lengths, including Ironman competitions. Rick is a quadriplegic with cerebral palsy, due to oxygen deprivation at birth. When he was 15 years old, he decided to participate in a five mile benefit run to raise money for a Lacrosse player who had been paralysed in an accident. He asked his father, Dick, who was no marathon runner, to push him in a wheelchair. After they completed their first run, Rick told his father how liberating the race made him feel. Team Hoyt has since completed over 70 marathons and 250 triathlons.

- **Iram Leon:** Diagnosed with terminal brain cancer in 2010, Iram decided he didn't want to give up running or spending time with his six-year old daughter. He has since completed six marathons while pushing his daughter in a stroller. Recently he came first in the Gusher Marathon in Texas, USA, with a time of three hours and seven minutes.

- **Allan Tyson:** In 2003, Allan fell off a bike when a dog crossed his path and ended up in a coma. When he woke up seven weeks later, he had to learn to walk, talk and everything else all over again. He knew it was a do or die situation and decided to get up and join a 20-week rehab program at New York University's Langone Medical Center. He ultimately realised that exercising was keeping him inspired and alive, and has since finished three New York City Marathons.

MY FINAL NOTES

We've spent a lot of time together, so I'd like say a few final words. Doing a marathon can be intimidating, whether you are walking or running. But this also makes a marathon one of the most rewarding activities you can do. I am always looking forward to my next one. Marathons have inspired me to live my life to the fullest and that includes constantly improving myself and appreciating the simple things in life such as good health and good friends.

I hope you are motivated to keep up with walking and will strive to live a marathon lifestyle. Before long, you may even end up joining a 100 Marathon Club.

Thanks for joining me on your journey. This book isn't the end of it. Do visit my website **www.marathonwalker.org** for continuous updates and articles.

I hope to see you on a marathon course some day!

Fi Hanafiah

17. REFERENCES

Additional information for anyone interested in walking and adopting the marathon lifestyle.

REFERENCES

Walker-friendly marathons

Canberra Walking Festival, Canberra, Australia
Columbus Marathon, Ohio, USA
Dublin Marathon, Dublin, Ireland
Fort4Fitness Seniors Marathon, Indiana, USA
Great Bermuda Walking Marathon, Hamilton, Bermuda
Honolulu Marathon, Hawaii, USA
Loch Ness Marathon, Scotland, United Kingdom
London Moonwalk, London, United Kingdom
Marine Corps Marathon, Virginia, USA
Melbourne Marathon, Melbourne, Australia
Mount Desert Island Marathon, Maine, USA
New York City Marathon, New York, USA
Ottawa Race Weekend, Ontario, Canada
Portland Marathon, Oregon, USA
Royal Victoria Marathon, British Columbia, Canada
San Diego Rock 'n' Roll Marathon, San Diego, USA
Sundown Marathon, Singapore

Note: Do confirm the marathon's cut-off time before you register as this could change from year to year.

Smartphone apps

Endomondo: GPS tracker (Android and iOS)
Calorie Counter by MyFitnessPal (Android and iOS)
Fitbit : For use with Fitbit devices (Android and iOS)

Garmin Connect: For use with Garmin devices (Android and iOS)
MapMyRun: GPS tracker (Android and iOS)
MapMyWalk: GPS tracker (Android and iOS)
Moves: Automatic activity tracker (Android and iOS)
Noom Coach: GPS tracker (Android and iOS)
Nike+ Running: GPS tracker (Android and iOS)
Runkeeper: GPS tracker (Android and iOS)
RunStar: GPS tracker (Android and iOS)
Runtastic: GPS tracker (Android and iOS)
Softrace: GPS tracker (Android and iOS)
Strava Running: GPS tracker (Android and iOS)

Note: Most of these apps are free. Those apps that require payment usually have a free version that you can try out first.

Gadgets, clothing & accessories

Fitbit: www.fitbit.com
Garmin: buy.garmin.com
Nike: store.nike.com
Patagonia: www.patagonia.com
Polar: www.polar.com
Road Runner Sports: www.roadrunnersports.com
The Ultra Marathon Running Store:
www.ultramarathonrunningstore.com
Under Armour: www.underarmour.com

Resources for women

Best Sports Bras for Runners (Runner's World article):
http://bit.ly/1huBsXz

Owner's Manual for the Female Runner (Runner's World article): http://bit.ly/1e0MIJ9
RunnerGirl (online resources): www.runnergirl.com
Uber Mother Runner (online resources): www.ubermotherrunner.com
Women's Running Clothes: http://bit.ly/1jugLzF

Resources for seniors

Hal Higdon's training plan for seniors: http://bit.ly/13uoIxQ
The Senior Walker (articles): http://abt.cm/1AFDFKS
Fort4Fitness Seniors Marathon: http://bit.ly/19ifhEo
Senior Living (article): http://bit.ly/1ciQVKZ

Websites

AIMS: Association of International Marathons and Distance Races: www.aimsworld.org
AIMS races calendar: www.aimsworldrunning.com/Calendar.htm
Find my Marathon: www.findmymarathon.com
IAAF (International Association of Athletics Federations): www.IAAF.org
Marathon Guide: www.marathonguide.com
Marathon Tour and Travel: www.marathontours.com
Runner's World: www.runnersworld.com
World Marathon Challenge: www.savethechildren.org.uk/wmc
World Marathon Majors: www.worldmarathonmajors.com

Happy Walking!

Photo credits

- Cover: Photodune (Extended Licence)
- Pexels.com
- http://commons.wikimedia.org/wiki/File%3ATwo-girls-exercising-cayucos-beach.jpg - "Mike" Michael L. Baird [CC BY 2.0 (http://creativecommons.org/licenses/by/2.0)], via Wikimedia Commons
- http://commons.wikimedia.org/wiki/File%3ASkyttis_athletics_tracks.jpg - by Petey21 (Own work) [Public domain], via Wikimedia Commons
- http://commons.wikimedia.org/wiki/File%3AMarcha_atletica_Perdida_Contacto_1.JPG - by Сидик из ПТУ [CC BY-SA 3.0 (http://creativecommons.org/licenses/by-sa/3.0)], via Wikimedia Commons
- http://commons.wikimedia.org/wiki/File%3AUS_Navy_070617-N-4774B-163_Runners_pass_the_starting_line_of_the_8.2_mile_Low_Tide_Ride_and_Stride_race_from_Imperial_Beach-to-Coronado%2C_California.jpg - U.S. Navy photo by Mass Communication Specialist 3rd Class Daniel A. Barker [Public domain], via Wikimedia Commons
- http://upload.wikimedia.org/wikipedia/commons/6/6d/Marahon_shoes.jpg - by Josiah Mackenzie [CC BY 2.0 (http://creativecommons.org/licenses/by/2.0)], via Wikimedia Commons
- http://commons.wikimedia.org/wiki/File%3AAddison's_Walk%2C_Winter_2002_(2).jpg - by Miles underwood at en.wikipedia [CC BY-SA 2.5 (http://creativecommons.org/licenses/by-sa/2.5)], from Wikimedia Commons
- http://commons.wikimedia.org/wiki/File%3AStretching_1200823.jpg - by Nevit Dilmen (Own work) [GFDL (http://www.gnu.org/copyleft/fdl.html), CC-BY-SA-3.0 (http://creativecommons.org/licenses/by-sa/3.0/) or CC BY-SA 2.5-2.0-1.0 (http://creativecommons.org/licenses/by-sa/2.5-2.0-1.0)], via Wikimedia Commons
- http://commons.wikimedia.org/wiki/File%3ATreadmills_at_gym.jpg - by U.S. Air Force Photo/Staff Sgt Araceli Alarcon [Public domain], via Wikimedia Commons
- http://commons.wikimedia.org/wiki/File%3AConchiglie_Pasta_Texture.jpg - by freestock.ca [CC BY-SA 3.0 (http://creativecommons.org/licenses/by-sa/3.0)], via Wikimedia Commons
- http://commons.wikimedia.org/wiki/File%3ARunning_Man_Kyle_Cassidy.jpg - by Kyle Cassidy (Email) [CC BY-SA 3.0 (http://creativecommons.org/licenses/by-sa/3.0)], via Wikimedia Commons
- http://commons.wikimedia.org/wiki/File%3APrague_Marathon_2013.JPG - by David Sedlecký (Own work) [CC BY-SA 3.0 (http://creativecommons.org/licenses/by-sa/3.0)], via Wikimedia Commons
- http://commons.wikimedia.org/wiki/File%3AWalking_for_Health_in_Epsom-5Aug2009_(2).jpg - by Walking for Health Paul Glendell / Natural England (originally posted to Flickr as WfH Epsom Aug 09_14) [CC BY-SA 2.0 (http://creativecommons.org/licenses/by-sa/2.0)], via Wikimedia Commons
- http://commons.wikimedia.org/wiki/File%3AThinking_Man.jpg - by د خالد تصف هذ (Own work) [CC BY-SA 4.0 (http://creativecommons.org/licenses/by-sa/4.0)], via Wikimedia Commons

Made in the USA
San Bernardino, CA
28 August 2016